This book belongs to

Stanley Cook

THE CHANNEL ISLANDS
An Archaeological Guide

The
CHANNEL ISLANDS
An Archaeological Guide

DAVID E. JOHNSTON

PHILLIMORE

1981

Published by
PHILLIMORE & CO. LTD.
London and Chichester

Head Office: Shopwyke Hall,
Chichester, Sussex, England

ISBN 0 85033 395 4

Printed and bound in Great Britain
by Billing and Sons Limited
Guildford, London, Oxford, Worcester

CONTENTS

LIST OF PLATES

(between pages 48 and 49)

LIST OF TEXT FIGURES

NOTE ON ILLUSTRATIONS

Plate 33 is reproduced by courtesy of La Société Jersiaise, drawings by Lukis (pls. 10, 11, 12 and 13 and figs. 13, 41 and 58) were photographed by Mr. W. Tipping and are the copyright of the States of Guernsey and the Guernsey Museum. Pl. 34 is reproduced by courtesy of the Alderney Society and Museum. Pl. 19 is by Mr. E. Sirett. The remaining photographs are by the author.

Many of the plans are from sources that show the monuments in better condition than they are in today; in some cases Lukis' measurements have been used to adjust his sketch plans. Wherever possible, the opportunity has been taken, for the first time, to redraw the plans to a common scale and orientation. The following conventions have been adopted: uprights and masonry in solid black, capstones outlined with dashes, displaced stones in outline and outcropping rock or doubtful stones in a dotted line. Figs. 4, 5 and 6 are the copyright of the St. Brelade Research Project; figs. 3 and 22 are by Maj. N. L. V. Rybot, and fig. 13 by Col. T. W. M. de Guérin; for the tailpiece to Part 1 (p. 59) thanks are due to Mr. Guppy and the Guernsey Evening Press. All other drawings are by the author. BKS Air Surveys Ltd. are acknowledged for the use of their map for fig. 60.

FOREWORD

The archaeological richness of the Channel Islands has long been recognized. Lying close to the French mainland on one of the principal routes which bound the communities occupying the Atlantic coasts of Europe together, the Islands have been subjected to influences from far afield, and yet at the same time they have maintained their own distinct cultural characteristics. For the archaeologist they provide a microcosm of Prehistoric society, their very insularity giving them an unusual potential as an archaeological study area.

Earlier this century Thomas Kendrick and Jacquetta Hawkes summed up the archaeology of the Channel Islands for a fast-growing archaeological audience. Since then two significant changes have taken place: the rate of archaeological discovery has rapidly increased, largely due to the active involvement of the Islanders themselves in their prehistory, while at the same time a more interested and widely-informed public have been visiting the Islands: for many of them the attractions of the past outweigh the lure of the beaches.

David Johnston's archaeological guide is a timely publication. His intimate knowledge of the region over a number of years and his own programmes of fieldwork ensure that this authoritative and up-to-date survey will be as valuable to the interested visitor as it will to the professional archaeologist.

BARRY W. CUNLIFFE

Oxford
July 1981

INTRODUCTION

Archaeological discoveries in the Channel Islands have advanced to the point where a definitive account might seem beyond the pen of a single author; and in a sense this book has been written by many people, although it has been put together by one. For archaeology in the Islands has reached a peak of activity in recent years, and those who are most active, in the museums and in the field, have little time to write books about it. Yet the players, we are told, see only a part of the game; and so it falls to myself, after some twelve years of lecturing, excavation and fieldwork in the Islands and on both sides of the Channel, to bring a more European perspective to the task and to attempt a disinterested review of progress. Not entirely disinterested, perhaps, as a proposal from the Islands in 1968 for a fresh study of their megalithic tombs soon developed into a programme of personal research. This initial encouragement has led to some original material in the first part of this book.

Part 1, therefore, is a summary account of our understanding of the archaeology of the Islands as it stood in 1980, and such is the pace of current research that it will soon be out of date. Part 2, on the other hand, is a description of what we hope will never change—a display of monuments whose preservation is unmatched in most parts of Europe today. It is these, together with three fine museums, that so impress the visitor. Every site has therefore been examined afresh, some have been re-excavated and many re-surveyed or studied for the first time since the two Bailiwicks were described in 1928 and 1939 by T. D. Kendrick and J. Hawkes. Their joint work, *The Archaeology of the Channel Islands,* is still an indispensable work for the serious student.

Nevertheless, there have been some deliberate omissions from this book. The observant reader will notice that some sites mentioned in Part 1 are missing from Part 2, and that some sensitive information, particularly the find-spots of coin hoards and metal objects, has been suppressed. This, unfortunately, is a sign of the times; for the archaeological resources of the Islands that have for so many centuries survived the pressures of agriculture, quarrying and urban development are now being increasingly pilfered by treasure-hunters with metal-detectors. This is more than pilfering: it is theft. And what is more, archaeological evidence is disappearing for ever, even when the objects themselves are reported. A true story from Jersey will illustrate the point. An unattended excavation was visited by a treasure-hunter whose metal-detector revealed a corroded iron object in an unexcavated part of the site. Disappointed, perhaps, that it was not worth keeping, he handed it in with information on its position. However, without noticing it he seems to have displaced an even more important sherd of pottery that was subsequently found loose in the mess. So a crucial piece of dating evidence was lost, and the treasure-hunter himself gained nothing. He is probably still unaware of the damage he did. A book of this kind inevitably brings these sites to the attention of guilty and innocent alike, and is published with some misgivings, particularly on the part of these whose job it is to look after the sites. Current legislation that is being drafted in the Islands represents some progress, and already, in Jersey, metal-detectors are banned from all lands administered by the States, the Société Jersiaise and the National Trust for Jersey. But legislation is merely a partial answer; only public opinion can being the problem under control in the long run, and we sincerely trust that readers of this book will play their part in protecting sites whose vulnerability is part of their appeal. We hope, in fact, that visitors will feel encouraged to visit those monuments that are accessible to the public and to obtain permission, where indicated, for those that are not. Public rights of way do not exist in the United Kingdom sense, and many sites are on private land; in these cases it is essential to ask permission first. Moreover, in Jersey, Guernsey and Sark almost every inch is cultivated. So a proper regard to gates, litter, and interference with agriculture and privacy is important in ensuring a welcome on remote sites where tourists are seldom seen.

Visitors, in fact, are always charmed by the friendliness of these Islands, described by Victor Hugo as 'fragments of France which have fallen into the sea and been picked up by England'. This is historically true, and English has long been the dominant language. But that is all: politically, economically and culturally the Channel Islands are independent of the British Government and of each other. The work that is described here is largely that of the people themselves, Island by Island, and describing it would have been impossible without the active co-operation of individual members of La Société Jersiaise, La Société Guernesiaise, the Alderney Society, and La Société Sercquiaise—as well as those Islanders, too numerous to name, whose hospitality and help in the field have made it possible.

I would like to thank all who have discussed their sites and allowed me to use their, often unpublished, material; and especially those who have been kind enough to read parts of the text in draft. For the foreword, and for much encouragement, I am grateful to Professor B. W. Cunliffe; and for other assistance to Professors P-R. Giot, J. L'Helgouach and the late Professor C. B. McBurney; to Drs. R. Jacobi, D. Hill, A. E. Mourant, and S. Shennan; to Mrs. M. B. Finlaison, Mrs. R. Cole, Mr. V. Coysh and Mr. and Mrs. K. Wilson; to Messrs. A. M. ApSimon, S. Briggs, R. B. Burns, J. Stevens Cox, D. A. Hinton, R. Keen, the Archaeology Branch of the Ordnance Survey, the Librarian of the Society of Antiquaries of London, the Librarian and staff of the Priaulx Library and staff of all the Museums for access to their collections; to the late Dame Sibyl Hathaway, Mr. M. Beaumont, Sir Charles Hayward, and Major A. G. Wood for so hospitably introducing me to their particular islands.

I owe a great debt to Dr. J. T. Renouf for help with the geological section, the illustrations and substance of which are derived largely from his work; and to Dr. P. Callow, who explained to me the complexities of La Cotte de St. Brelade, and provided illustrations. Dr. I. Kinnes has helped me similarly with his current excavations at Les Fouaillages. Dr. R. Kellett-Smith kindly allowed me to use his unpublished history of Herm, the manuscript of which is in the Priaulx Library.

I must thank Mr. W. F. Tipping of Guernsey and the Department of Teaching Media of Southampton University for invaluable photographic assistance, and Mr. E. Sirett for the new photograph in pl. 19; Mr. A. Johnston for a new, professional survey of The Nunnery, Alderney; *The Guernsey Evening Press* and Mr. Guppy for the drawing on p. 59, the University of Southampton for generous leave of absence and for practical assistance with my research; and my family for their forbearance during my frequent absences for fieldwork and excavation—or simply for writing and drawing the illustrations for this book.

The publishers, Messrs. Phillimore, have been unfailingly helpful and supportive at all stages in the preparation and production of this volume, and I am deeply grateful to them. This said, I must stress that what follows is a personal synthesis, and that the views and interpretations are not necessarily those of the publishers, or of the individuals and Societies that have helped me. The responsibility for the errors that remain is, of course, mine.

DAVID E. JOHNSTON

SOUTHAMPTON
November, 1980

'LIGHTLY TREAD'

Where'er you walk, fine Flints shall meet the eye.
Beneath these Mounds sharp Arrow-heads do lie.
Where'er you tread, the precious things shall gleam.
Come, LUKIS! hasten and your time redeem.

Found among the Lukis papers in Guernsey Museum

PART 1

THE ARCHAEOLOGICAL BACKGROUND

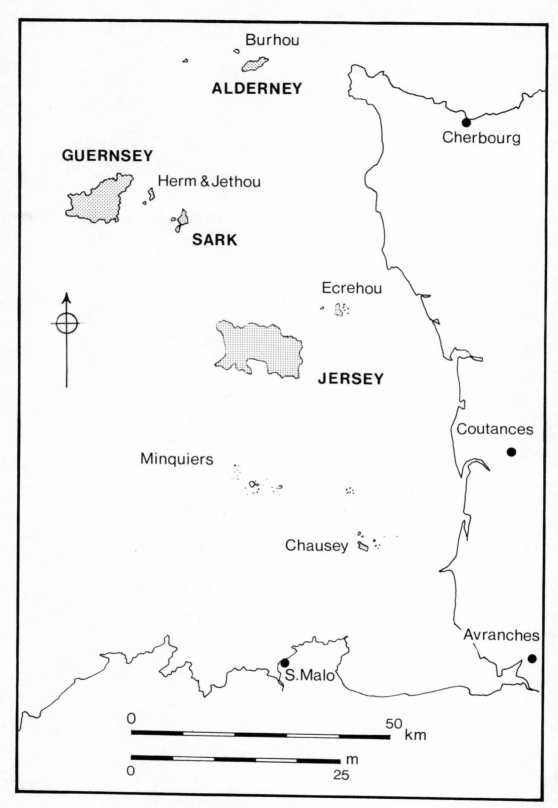

Fig. 1. The Channel Islands.

THE SHAPING OF THE ISLANDS

THIS BOOK IS AN ACCOUNT of the interplay of man and his environment. The story is a long one, and man enters to play his part only in the later stages; in them, he was both witness and participant, exploiting his environment not only to secure his own survival but also to build the monuments that are the historical evidence of his success.

We must start with the rocks, for these are the substructure to soils, vegetation and wildlife, and the source of the tools in stone and metal with which the landscape was tamed. The oldest rocks in the Channel Islands are among the oldest known in the British Isles and France, dating back some 2,500 million years. They are the *Icart Gneiss* and other similar rocks, formed by great pressure deep in the earth's crust from even older strata solidified from a molten mass. These are the so-called basement rocks of *Pentevrian* age, older than about 1,000 million years. The deposits of succeeding *Brioverian* time, down to about 700 million years ago, were largely marine sediments. However, towards the end of the Brioverian a new feature appeared —a series of volcanoes, apparently in the sea-bed off what is now Jersey, creating the only true volcanic rocks to be found in the Channel Islands today. This marked the beginning of the period when the whole of Armorica was rent by convulsions of the earth's hard crust. This is the *Cadomian* orogenic (or 'mountain-forming') cycle of convulsions. Massive dome-shaped swellings of molten magma like bubbles forced their way upward into the crust. The first were chemically basic *gabbros* that in places were severely altered by later intrusions of new granites. Significant mountains formed over parts of the Channel Islands area and their erosion by wind and water under desert-like conditions produced the coarse pudding-mix of pebbles and boulders that is the Rozel Conglomerate of Jersey. Finer gravels, sands and silts were washed out to sea and formed the Alderney Sandstones. In the shallow seas that covered much of Armorica marine live thrived.

The shallow seas following the Cadomian orogeny persisted for several hundred million years, an era here as elsewhere noted for its abundant and diverse forms of marine life and perhaps, above all, for the conquest of land by plant and animal.

By 250 million years ago, a further series of convulsions had welded rocks new and old into a single unit. This unit, though not geographically the Armorica of today, possessed most of the fundamental geological structure which still characterises the rocks beneath the islands, rocks which were to provide prehistoric man with very beautiful, fine-grained and colourful stones for axes and ornaments. These rocks, moreover, are the source of most of the building materials for the monuments described in this book.

Internal movements did not cease 250 million years ago; it was merely that Armorica was no longer at the centre of major earth-building processes. One of

1

the more important of these processes involved the splitting of the then narrow Atlantic ocean and the beginning of the fundamental separation of the old and new worlds along the line of the mid-Atlantic volcanic ridge (Iceland, Azores, etc.). The separation of the continents, or plates as they are technically known, set up major stresses along the edge of the adjacent continents and Armorica was one of those areas much affected by faulting—the movement of one area of land with respect to another, vertically or horizontally or in any combination. Such faults and erosional processes initiated the coastline patterns of Armorica as we know it now, notably causing the formation of the English Channel and the shallow embayment of the Normanno-Breton gulf in which the Channel Islands present peaks and plateaux.

At a comparatively early period in this sequence, some 65–130 million years ago, the famous Chalk deposits were laid down on the bottom of warm seas over much of England and France. Deposits of Chalk off the Guernsey coast contain abundant flint, the rock so highly prized by prehistoric man.

Laid down beneath the sea, the flint of the Chalk deposits off Guernsey would never have been accessible to man—whose appearance on the scene was still most of that 70 million years away—had it not been for the events of the most recent period of the earth's geological story, the *Quaternary*. This period is divided into two epochs, the *Pleistocene* (down to 10,000 years ago) and the *Recent* (the last 10,000 years).

Several million years ago, before the Quaternary began in fact, the climate was beginning to deteriorate. Eventually the world was plunged into the first of the Pleistocene ice ages, and a series of severe climatic oscillations has persisted since. Each glaciation was matched by a warmer (or rather, less cold) interglacial, the fluctuations being measured in thousands rather than millions of years. The character of these phases, like the terminology, varies from one part of Europe to another; the great ice-sheets that formed did not cover all parts, and conditions in the Channel Islands, in particular, were periglacial—that is, outside the area of ice cover.

The ebb and flow of the ice-sheets affected the sea-levels dramatically, as the water was alternately evaporated to nourish the ice build-up and then released during the warmer interglacials. The land not actually covered by ice received the melt water that flowed violently during spring melt over it, depositing both coarse gravels and finer sands and silts. As the silts dried they were picked up by the strong winds and carried immense distances before coming to rest. Much of this wind-borne dust, originating in distant parts of Europe and even beyond, settled to become the familiar *loess* of the Channel Islands. During the colder phases of each glaciation frost wedged loose large masses of rock; in the wet periods of the year water and gravity washed them down to mix with the finer silt and loess to form clayey, rubbly *head*. This is the final phase of the landscape-shaping over the 2–3 million years or so of the Pleistocene, when the peaks, plateaux and valleys of northern Europe were sculpted into their present forms. The process was virtually complete by the end of the last glaciation, the *Devensian*, about 10,000 years ago, and the loesses of this final phase are today the fertile, loamy soils of Jersey, Guernsey and Sark.

During the Pleistocene, the level of the oceans rose and fell more or less in phase with interglacial and glacial phases. The shape of past shorelines in the Normanno-Breton embayment, associated with ocean level changes, can be roughly drawn using a map showing sea depths (Admiralty charts, etc.). Recent scientific advances have

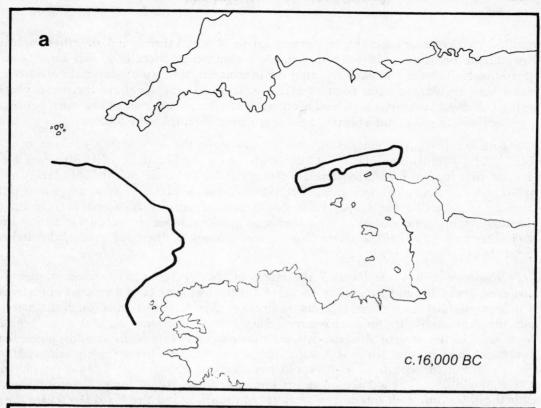

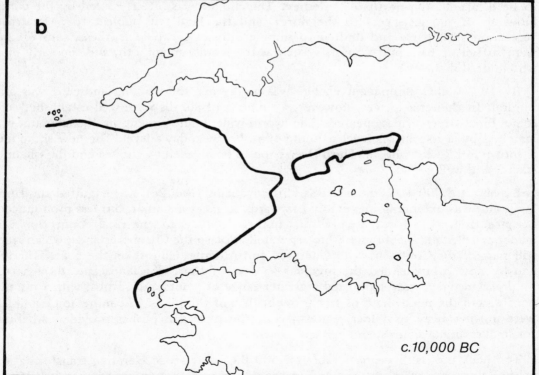

Fig. 2. Stages in the formation of the English Channel (redrawn from Renouf and Urry 1976).

enabled particular sea depths to be related to specific times, and so maps such as Fig. 2 can be drawn. It must be stressed that such shorelines and timings are approximations only, and each represents one moment during a process of intermittent, rather than regular, advance (or retreat). At one and 11 metres above the present high spring tide level, wave-cut notches, often associated with beaches of sea-worn pebbles, mark periods of still stand of interglacial seas higher than those of today.

Before we leave the glaciations, we should note the appearance of man in the record. The penultimate glaciation, the *Wolstonian* (earlier than 120,000 years ago) saw the first known habitation levels in Jersey at La Cotte de St. Brelade. Jersey was in no sense an island at this time, but rather a rocky plateaux with caves in a flat, desolate, tundra-like landscape. Flint could still be readily obtained at this stage, although from some distance. The archaeological evidence from La Cotte for this and subsequent *Palaeolithic* (Old Stone Age) phases is discussed more fully below (pp. 8-14).

Following the low sea level of the latest of the ice ages, the Devensian, the sea advanced gradually and irregularly to flood for the last time (if the present interglacial is indeed the last—and there is every indication that it is not!) the English Channel and the Normanno-Breton embayment. Stages in this process are shown in Fig. 2. Early man in the area of the islands would have been a witness of the advancing sea, though change in one lifetime would not normally have been readily appreciable. Fig. 2a shows the coastline as it would have looked about 16,000 B.C. and during several stages of earlier ice ages. The sea level was some 100m. lower than at present, with the shore line well out in the Western Approaches and the Hurd Deep presumed to be a lake to the north of Alderney. The climate was bitter, cooled by the winds blowing off the ice-sheets to the north, and the land still subject to permafrost. vegetation was sparse and limited to summer mosses and lichens; these, surprisingly, were sufficient to support animals, such as the woolly mammoth, and the early men who hunted them.

By 10,000 B.C. permanent change was in the air, though the landscape was still tundral. In sheltered places, however, a number of shrubs were well established and some birch trees had appeared. The world-wide improvement in the climate was matched by a rise in sea level to some 40m. below today's level. The new shore-line is shown in Fig. 2b, with the Hurd Deep soon to be invaded by the sea and the Channel Islands still well inland.

By about 8,500 B.C. the sea was still advancing (Fig. 2c), had engulfed the Hurd Deep and was extending inexorably eastwards to meet a similar, but less pronounced, advance from the North Sea; within another 1,000 years the final connection was made, and Britain and France were separated. Not so the Channel Islands, which were still part of the Continent with Guernsey and Alderney almost on the coast. The sea had by now overwhelmed the precious sources of flint. The landscape, though still tundral and open, now supported a greater range of plants and shrubs, with fruit and berries, and the next phase of tree growth, that of the pines. The more arctic animals were moving away to colder regions, while the trees and bushes provided a habitat for smaller animals, birds, and herds of deer.

The next thousand years, to about 7,500 B.C., saw an accelerating transformation in the landscape, which by the end of the period was predominantly wooded. Minor climatic fluctuations still continued and in some parts of Europe fierce winter gales

4

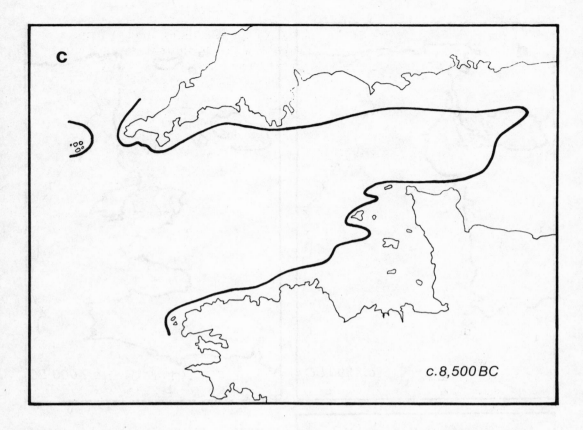

c.8,500 BC

flattened whole forests which in warmer, wetter conditions slowly turned to peat bogs. Occasionally the actual trees can be recognised in these early peat deposits, though more usually only the pollen survives. The identifiable pollen grains thus provide us with a sequence of vegetational development and tell us that hazel, oak and alder now made their appearance, to be followed by other deciduous trees. New varieties of deer, wild horse and pig were some of the animals that man, adapting himself to the new environment, added to his now varied diet. The archaeological evidence for this *Mesolithic* phase is elaborated below (pp. 15–18). The coastline still looks unfamiliar (Fig. 2d), though Guernsey can be recognised as a pensinula connected to the mainland by a tenuous isthmus.

By about 7,000 B.C. Alderney, Guernsey and Sark were islands at last, and at low tide the sea must have been dotted with reefs (Fig. 2e). Large tidal estuaries were forming to the north and south of what were to become Jersey and the Minquiers. In places the water was quite deep and strong currents were rapidly eroding and shaping the new islands. The pollen record tells us that there were thick deciduous forests with oak predominating, though alder, lime, elm and many others were numerous. Birch and pine, preferring a colder climate and sandy soils, were in rapid decline. Wind-blown sand was accumulating near the shore with exposed headlands gathering gorse and heather.

Our last map (Fig. 2f) shows the position at the beginning of the *Neolithic* period, about 4000 B.C. The sea level was roughly that of today's extreme low tide. Jersey, Herm and Jethou were now islands; the Ecrehous, Minquiers and Chausey Islands were still lowland areas covered with forest and other vegetation, sporadically inhabited by

5

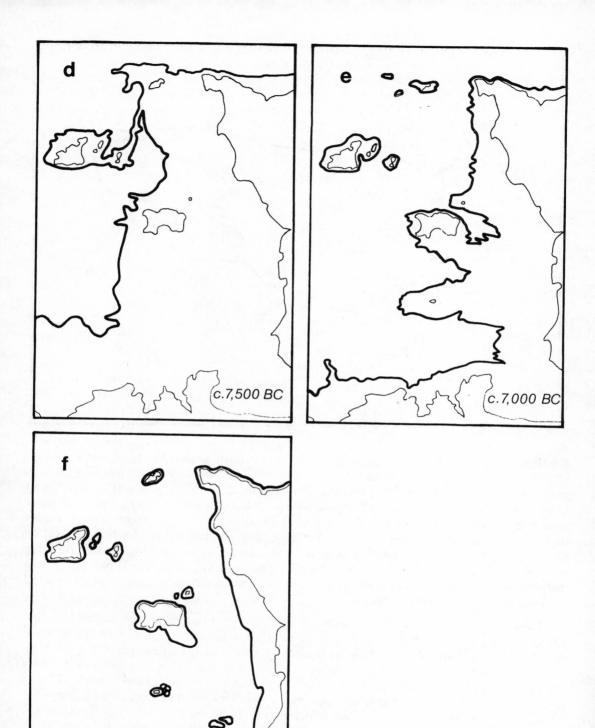

Fig. 2 (contd., see p. 3)

man. The final shaping of today's coastline (Fig. 1) was not yet complete; archaeologically, the insularity of the island communities was already beginning to show, and we might briefly mention something comparable in the animal world. In 1939 several bones found in the 8m. raised beach in Jersey were recognised (Zeuner, 1940, 1946) as belonging to a new but extinct race of deer. Of roe or fallow deer size, but possessing bones of unusual proportions, it was named *Cervus elaphus jerseyensis* Zeuner. It seems to represent a dwarf insular race of *Cervus elaphus* evolved on Jersey during a period of isolation in the last, or *Ipswichian*, interglacial—some 120,000 years ago.

The peat beds mentioned above are encountered from time to time around the coasts when deep holes are dug or soundings taken. The best-known exposures appear at low tide in St. Ouen's Bay, Jersey, in the shape of a 'submerged forest' (plate 3). Oak, hazel and alder have been identified, and in a particularly spectacular exposure in 1902 (Sinel, 1909) some 500 tree-stumps were counted. It does continue under the sand-dunes nearby, though its relationship to other peat beds elsewhere in the island is uncertain. The circumstances governing peat formation were often strictly local, and this is borne out by the complicated sequence in the St. Helier basin. Dunlop (1896) identified two peat layers separated by a marine clay deposit and overlying alluvial and marine clays. The base of the sequence was gravel. This was recorded in the site of the gas works, where in 1952 the sequence could be related to a newly-revealed cist and associated stone avenue (Wedgwood and Mourant, 1954). The structures appeared to have been built upon the equivalent of the lower peat layer, on firm ground in drier conditions; the cist was subsequently submerged by the sea and filled with more peaty deposits, and finally the whole disappeared under more mud and a thick layer of the upper peat. This sequence, however, could not be entirely correlated with the nearby 1896 section, in which unworn flint chips were found on the gravel base and a polished neolithic axe of dolerite, pottery and bovine teeth in the lower peat. This is not, incidentally, the only prehistoric tomb in such a low-lying, coastal situation; that at Oyster Point, Herm (p. 118), is today on the beach.

Recognising the prehistoric land-surface is, of course, an essential part of any archaeological excavation, and in the Channel Islands it frequently appears under considerable depths of blown sand. This is so, too, in the nearer parts of Brittany and Normandy, where the conditions are broadly the same. In Jersey, the neolithic and Bronze Age land-surface at the Blanches Banques and elsewhere lies on a bed of compact ferrugineous sand of much earlier date. Fierce sandstorms in the Bronze Age are attested by the pot found upright, filled with limpet-shells, overwhelmed and abandoned in one such storm (p. 37). Similar prehistoric deposits are recorded elsewhere in Jersey, for instance at Ville-ès-Nouaux (pp. 75-7), and Green Island (p. 75). Another prehistoric horizon below more recent sand was identified in Alderney at Les Pourciaux South. In parts of Brittany the sand-deposits are often of Iron Age, or more often medieval, date. Legends of medieval cataclysms abound, and the Alderney tradition that the Old Town of Longis was overwhelmed in a single night is typical. Both the prehistoric and medieval sand-deposits are discussed by Keen (1975) and Ranwell (1975), who quote a documentary account of 1495 (pp. 422-3). The Alderney story is supported by the excavation (unpublished) at the Kennels, on Longy Common, where two deep deposits of blown sand were separated by a buried soil, presumed to be medieval, with apparent signs of ploughing; and not far away pottery of the 9th or 10th centuries A.D. (p. 53) has been found 2.5m. deep in this sand.

PALAEOLITHIC MAN

The first Men in the Channel Islands make a modest appearance in the archaeological record with two unsophisticated flint implements (Fig. 3). The lower was found on the beach at Havre des Pas, Jersey, as was probably the other. Both have an orange ochreous staining, and both have been severely rolled by wave-action. They have probably travelled some way from an early raised beach and certainly cannot be taken as evidence for the first human occupation of the caves. They are simple hand-axes, flaked on both surfaces and can be assigned to the *Acheulean* phase of the Lower Palaeolithic; they cannot be precisely dated, but could be as old as *c.* 600,000 B.C. Their makers were probably representatives of the earliest class of true man, *Homo erectus*, a creature whose developed bone-structure and upright gait distinguishes him from the more evolved man-like apes. He gathered food from a desolate landscape with little vegetation and hunted arctic animals such as the mammoth and woolly rhinoceros. Throughout all or most of the Palaeolithic period (that is, up to the end of the last Ice Age) the Islands were part of the mainland (Figs. 2c, 2d), though Jersey will have been cut off during the interglacials. So there is no good reason why evidence for early man should not turn up elsewhere than in Jersey; indeed, a single flake found recently in Alderney and identified as

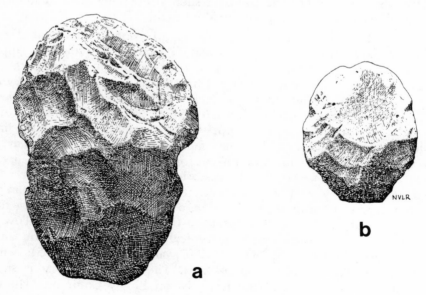

a

b

Fig. 3.   Two Acheulean flint handaxes from Jersey x ½ (drawing by
N. L. V. Rybot).

possibly palaeolithic emphasises the point. Jersey, however, possesses the only inhabited caves known so far, though other sites, such as rock shelters, may be masked by the head or even under the sea. In Jersey, isolated finds are reported from time to time, and are summarised by Keen (1978: add also *Annu. Bull. Soc. Jersiaise* 22, 1980, 374). They come mostly from the western end of the Island where the inhabited caves and the best exposures of Upper Pleistocene deposits are to be found.

The earliest signs of human occupation in Jersey are associated with a rise in sea-level that created the 18-metre raised beach and related wave-cut notches in the cliffs. The date of this beach is quite uncertain, as also is its place in the sequence of glaciations. One view sees it as a warm intermission in the penultimate glaciation, the Wolstonian; another stresses that such a rise in sea level implies the melting of a great quantity of ice, incompatible with a mere intermission (or *interstadial*). The exact relationship of the early Wolstonian to the preceding Hoxian is likely to be in need of revision, and the Jersey 18-metre episode may conceivably fit into the grey area between them.

The earliest occupation has been identified in two Jersey caves, La Cotte à la Chèvre and La Cotte de St. Brelade. The former has been cut into a weakness in the granite by wave-action at the 18-metre level, forming a deep, rather narrow cave, some 10m. in depth and about 3.6m. and 4.5m. in height and breadth, becoming somewhat narrower and lower towards the inner end. The most striking aspect of the cave today is the complete smoothing of the end of the cave by the repeated dashing against it of large rounded bounders which now sit there like the peas in a in a referee's whistle. Occupation evidence has been known since 1861, on a loess deposited upon a bed of sand and pebbles (Sinel and Nicolle, 1912). By 1964, however, it was realised that the age of the implements did not tally with the much greater age of the 18-metre level, and a further excavation by McBurney (1967,

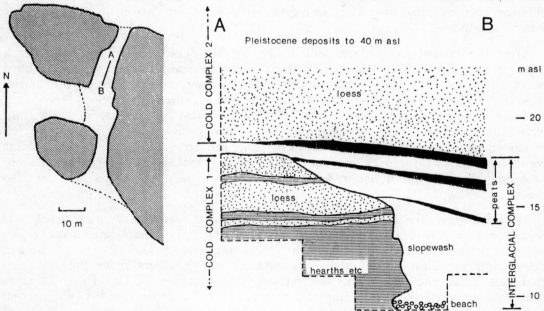

Fig. 4. La Cotte de St. Brelade, Jersey, simplified plan and section (by courtesy of the St. Brelade Research Project).

9

223-4) discovered a lower loess with an earlier, different, flint industry. This older leoss rests on the raised beach. The date, then, of this first occupation is related to our understanding of the lower loess, whose deposition must be earlier than 130,000 B.C.

This simple sequence has much in common with the far more complex story at La Cotte de St. Brelade, as revealed by a long series of excavations. The cave to-day is a T-shaped junction of two ravines (Fig. 4a) with an over-arching rock bridge at B. At high tide the sea enters the western arm and has already removed a substantial quantity of the deposits laid down there during the last glaciation. It is not even certain that it was a true cave in palaeolithic times; all that we can say is that during the time that it became completely filled with deposits, natural and artificial, it was probably a partly roofed fissure providing much of its shelter through the overhang that resulted from non-vertical jointing in the rock. This was probably a more effective overhang than today. The excavations have shown that throughout its history the fluctuations in temperature have loosened blocks from the roof and walls, causing rock-falls that must have made habitation perilous. The final stage in this disintegration came on 3 September 1915, when the wall of head deposits that had been mistaken for solid rock at the back of the cave collapsed, and the nine excavators escaped with their lives.

A simplified section of these deposits in the north ravine is given in Fig. 4b, from which the numerous large granite boulders have been omitted for clarity. The principal layers of human occupation are shaded, and originally extended some distance to the south. The complex of hearths and loess (Cold Complex 1) was laid down during the *Wolstonian* (penultimate) glaciation. During the last interglacial (*Ipswichian*) it was brought to an end by a return of the sea to the 8-metre level. Although this was lower than the floor-level at the time, wave-action undermined and cut away the greater part of the deposits to some distance inside the cave, resulting in a rather unstable cliff (or 'cornice'), just over 16m. in height, with beach deposits at its base. The cave was now abandoned by man.

After the retreat of the sea, still during the Ipswichian interglacial, the beach deposits were covered by slumped material from the earlier layers, and later by a series of peats. The slopewash so formed contained artifacts from the earlier deposits, a fact that misled the earlier excavators; their meticulous recording, however, has enabled many of these finds to be distinguished from those that were found in their primary stratified positions. The deposits of the first Cold Complex produced an important and varied series of stone industries, some of whose products we discuss below. Moreover, in each of the two principal layers of loess immediately preceding the interglacial rise in sea-level were found the 'bone-heaps' that are also described below.

The last great glaciation, the *Devensian,* caused a further fall in sea-level, and re-united Jersey with the mainland for the last time. The complicated stratigraphy of the further deposits of head and loess interleaved with layers of human occupation (at least 11 in the later phases) and boulders from the relentless rock-falls inside the cave forms the second Cold Complex of Fig. 4b. Once more the cave sheltered parties of hunters, this time of the more evolved *Neanderthal* type (*Homo sapiens*) whose physical characteristics are fairly close to those of modern man. This final glaciation, in its three principal phases, covers the latest developments of the Palaeolithic in Europe. In France and Spain these include the flowering of cave art; in Jersey, however, the Upper Palaeolithic is (on present knowledge) utterly absent, the archaeological record ending temporarily in about 50,000 B.C. We may never know why La Cotte was finally abandoned at a time when occupation of other European caves is so well documented. A massive increase in the rock-falls is one likely factor, combined with further deposition of wind-borne loess and periglacial head, leaving very little room to live, or even to stand upright. Indeed, by the time that serious excavations started in 1910 the cave was virtually full, a total depth of some 50m. of deposits both natural and man-made.

There were thus two broad phases of human occupation, by no means continuous; they probably represent seasonal, or at least intermittent, habitation by fairly small groups of hunters and their families of some ten or a dozen individuals. The territory for hunting and food-gathering would be extensive, and the cave would be used as a base. This last point is dramatically borne out by the most remarkable and unexpected find of all, something unparalleled in Pleistocene Europe. At the back of the cave, in the layers attributed to the Wolstonian occupation of the first Cold Complex, at least two vast 'bone heaps' accumulated. On sites of this nature the food debris normally consists of very small splinters of bone broken open to extract the marrow; here were large quantities of large intact bones, mainly of mammoth and rhinoceros. By contrast, in La Cotte à la Chèvre all trace of bone had disappeared in the acidic soil; here it was probably the sheer quantity that ensured preservation. The remains of about 350 individual animals have been identified so far, and they lay superimposed in groups separated by layers of loess and at one point by flat slabs of rock. Different layers contained different heaps; in one the shoulder-blades were set in a geometric arrangement, in another were skulls placed with ribs alongside. One mammoth skull had a rib driven horizontally through it. All showed signs of injury, as though they had been killed by being driven over the cliff. They were not complete skeletons, but rather selected portions of the carcasses. One quite unproven suggestion is that they represent a 'cold store', in the prevailing low temperatures of the time, of meat for future consumption. Owl pellets found on the bones imply that the 'store' was eventually abandoned; perhaps the hunters perished and the meat became inedible?

When the long analysis of this material is complete it will give us an unrivalled glimpse of Middle Palaeolithic hunting, butchering and feeding habits. A further tantalising clue to the way of life of these earlier inhabitants of the cave is some lumps of scarlet ochre in the lowest levels. This is of too early a date to have been intended for painting the cave—though we have no idea of how they decorated their bodies—and we are reminded of the practice elsewhere, at a very early period, of including red ochre in burials of the dead. The meaning of these lumps, however, is quite uncertain. A further discovery, in the last season of excavation, was a hole with ashes in it and a flue; the meaning of this, too, is uncertain, but it may possibly have been for smoking meat.

Actual remains of man, of one or more individuals, have been found in the deposits. In 1954 a concentration of small fragments was found and provisionally published (Burdo, 1959, 73–4); 10 of these were identified as collar-bones, right ulna, left knee-cap, vertebra, and parts of skull. They may possibly belong to *Homo erectus,* but this is by no means certain. Fragments of the later inhabitants, *Homo sapiens neanderthalensis,* were also found in the earlier excavations: in 1915 two pieces of a child's skull (Angel and Coon, 1954), and, in 1910–11, 13 teeth in a jaw that was too decomposed to be recovered (Keith, 1912). This last discovery was

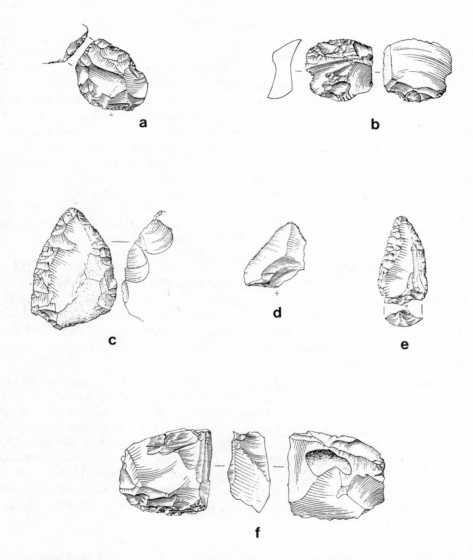

Fig. 5. Flint tools from the lowest occupation levels at La Cotte de St. Brelade x ½
(drawing by H. Martingell, courtesy of the St. Brelade Research Project).

one of the earliest finds of Neanderthal man in Europe, and was rightly celebrated at the time. None of these finds was a burial, and the 1954 fragments were charred and found with animal bones that were presumably food remains.

The stone implements illustrate particularly well the response to a changing environment; for the encroachment of the sea and the consequent loss of the flint sources is closely matched by an ever more economical treatment of the best flint and the use of less satisfactory stones, such as granite, dolerite, quartz and greenstone. These material constraints affect our understanding of the tools themselves in two ways: first, we must be cautious about wider cultural comparisons with other parts of the world (such as Africa, or the classic culture-sequence of France) where abundant flint allowed tool-forms to evolve differently. Second, this and other parallel analyses have suggested that many characteristics of palaeolithic industries can be related to special activities and are not necessarily indicators that particular points have been reached along an evolutionary path (McBurney and Callow, 1971, 201). With these reservations in mind, we can cautiously characterise the early levels at La Cotte de St. Brelade (those of the first Cold Complex) as *Pre-Mousterian,* the industry being predominantly concerned with flake-tools. In other words, their flint technology was more economical than that of their Acheulean predecessors; for, previously, in making a hand-axe as much as one third of the nodule would have disappeared as waste, whereas in the newer techniques the nodule was treated as a core from which flakes were detached to become in their turn the basis of implements. These two traditions were not exclusive, and at La Cotte a certain conservatism can be detected in the earliest levels. An early form of *cleaver,* for instance, common in Lower Palaeolithic deposits in Africa, but practically unknown north of the Loire, has been recognised. And in some of the early levels there are plenty of hand-axes of Acheulean type. What is characteristic of the new technology is the use of secondary retouch on the flake to produce tools for scraping and other operations. These are illustrated in Fig. 5, all tools from the Cambridge excavations (layer A, immediately below the lower of the two bone heaps) in the first of the two major cold complexes some time before 130,000 B.C. Except for *f* (a scraper made on a core) all are made by retouch on flakes, and show the very extensive secondary trimming on several edges and even on the butt in the case of *b.* With the exception of *d,* all the pieces are rather thick, with steep working edges suitable for scraping or planing. In the case of *d,* the weakness of the working edge precludes its use for heavy scraping tasks. The facetted butt of *e* should be noted; this resembles the *Levallois* technique, in which small flakes were removed from the core to prepare a striking platform at right-angles to the core-face before the flake was struck off.

The upper, later occupation (Cold Complex 2) was studied in the excavations at the beginning of this century. Only selected artifacts were kept and the associated material discarded. Even so, it is clear that it conformed broadly to that of *Mousterian* industries as commonly found in northern France. There was still a conservative element in the flintwork—the beautifully finished hand-axe of Fig. 6, for example, is in the Acheulean tradition, although it was found in the lowest of the later occupation levels (that is, from early in the last glaciation—the second of the major cold complexes). On open sites in northern Brittany there is a distinct industry of the Mousterian in the Acheulean tradition; for example, at Kervouster (Finistère), the hand-axes were small but numerous, many of them (if not all) apparently worked

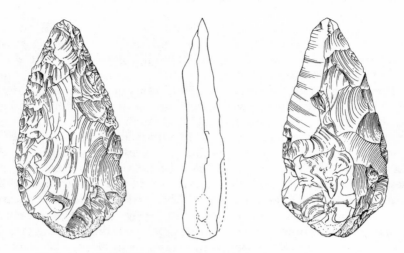

Fig. 6.   Flint hand-axe from the lowest occupation level of La Cotte
de St. Brelade x ½ (drawing by H. Martingell, courtesy of the
St. Brelade Research Project).

bifacially on substantial flakes, while the cleavers at Bois-du-Rocher were definitely flake-tools (Monnier, 1979, 106–110). On the other hand, some tools from the latest levels seem to show an anticipation of the long, thin blade techniques characteristic of the Upper Palaeolithic elsewhere in Europe. The simplicity of these tool forms belies a very advanced mastery of controlled flaking. We must admire the skill and ingenuity with which these men came to terms with a growing shortage of the essential materials. Detailed analysis of the later phases is now impossible, because the material was not preserved entire by the earlier excavators; the material from the Cambridge excavations, however, is being subjected to detailed statistical treatment (McBurney and Callow, 1971, 199–202). The waste flakes, it is clear, were being extensively used for tool-making, and the cores were worked down to the irreducible minimum. Even used tools were rejuvenated with up to three successive lines of retouch along the edges. In some, the final master-stroke was the removal of a clean flake by a vertical blow at one corner to produce a fresh working edge. The technique is akin to that for making a *burin,* or graver, and is by no means easy. But it was very common practice here, and the waste spalls are found in their hundreds. This technique is peculiar to La Cotte, and it represents a determined and ingenious response to the rather special circumstances.

The history of this long and complicated excavation is summarised below (p. 58), and the bibliography is correspondingly long. A useful account of the earliest work is by Marrett (1916) and Fr. Burdo published his work on the lowest levels (1959) before he relinquished the work. Some of his conclusions have had to be revised in the light of the later work, of which the latest summary (with bibliography) is that by McBurney and Callow (1971). The post-excavation work still continues, and the excavators have kindly allowed their current ideas (as yet unpublished) to be incorporated in this account, together with new drawings (Figs. 4–6) provided for the purpose.

MESOLITHIC SETTLERS

The end of the ice ages was not a sudden phenomenon, and developments at the end of the Upper Palaeolithic show that man was adapting himself successfully to the new environment over a long period. The major environmental changes occurred between about 8,300 and 5,000 B.C., and the principal change was the replacement of open tundra-like vegetation by forests. Pollen analysis has charted the changing nature of these forests, starting with the establishment of full birch cover over the whole of north-western Europe, the areas of open vegetation becoming progressively smaller. Pine appears next in the record, and for a period it seems to have completely replaced the birch in some areas. By about 7,000 B.C., however, pine was overtaken by hazel as the dominant tree species, its high frequency in some places suggesting partial forest clearance by man. By about 3,000 B.C. the record shows mixed oak forests with elm, alder and hazel.

The arctic animals had now retreated from Europe, and the temperate forests sheltered a variety of animals—red and roe deer, elk, pig, brown bear, and others—together with birds and fish in rivers and inland lakes. Exploitation of the new resources often required several different bases, with perhaps temporary or seasonal camp-sites in the less thickly wooded areas and open environments, or beside rivers and lakes and on the beach. Shellfish would be a dependable item in the diet that attracted some mesolithic groups to the coastal regions. The equipment for exploiting these new conditions was largely a development of Upper Palaeolithic types, such as bone and antler harpoons and fish-hooks (in Scandinavia and north Germany), flint-tipped arrowheads, scrapers and so on; organic materials have seldom survived anywhere, so we must imagine plenty of other equipment. Fish-nets and traps have survived in Russia and Denmark respectively, though we do not know if they formed part of the equipment of British or French mesolithic populations. Dug-out canoes have certainly survived in some parts of Europe, and there must have been tools for grubbing-out roots (rather than true cultivation). Very occasionally the camp-sites have been excavated, and in two classic sites—Téviec and Hoëdic in Brittany—burials grouped in cemeteries. These and other sites have confirmed the efficiency of mesolithic archery with the discovery of flint arrow-tips embedded in the spines of both aurochs and a human being. Unfortunately, we can only speculate about the meaning of the latter.

What is the evidence for this from the Channel Islands? Disappointingly little—indeed so little that it has been suggested that in the Islands (or at least Jersey) this phase is entirely absent (Hawkes, 1939, 3, 43-4). This, however, is probably a misconception, and there are two reasons for it. First, in view of the known rise in sea-level after the last glaciation, one would expect such sites to be in the lower, formerly coastal areas that are now under the sea—in other words, we have lost our sites. The distribution of supposed mesolithic sites in Guernsey demonstrates the strictly coastal nature of what has, apparently, survived—and, indeed, recent fieldwork on one of these has revealed a classic site with true *microliths* that shows that all is not lost. Second, microliths and tiny flints that could be mesolithic have been known for many years throughout the islands, but generally on sites where later material is also found. In fact, the Neolithic of the Channel Islands contains plenty of tiny flints that could easily be confused with true mesolithic artifacts. This is due to the wretched quality of the flint available—the sources of good flint were now lost for ever under the sea, and man had to be content with beach-pebble flint. This material, intractable even in expert hands, imparts a timeless quality to the results, many of which—in the Channel Islands at least—can be at home in any 'period' up to the Bronze Age. Some tool forms, that is, have a very long life, moreover, tiny flints can survive for thousands of years in the soil, to reappear confusingly in earthen monuments of a later date. A good example both of the confusion of dates and of the timeless problems of beach-pebble flint was provided by the excavation of the Tourgis Dolmen in Alderney. Here the soil scraped up in the late Bronze Age for the mound contained the waste from an earlier working-floor (neolithic or early Bronze Age) which the excavators found sealed beneath it (Johnston, 1974). There was some evidence that pebbles had been split open on one part of the site and that the suitable ones had been passed to another part for further working. A very high percentage had been rejected at once, and even then the great majority of the flakes struck from the rest (167 out of 267) preserved some of the original cortex, or crust, of the pebble. A series of hammer-stones of different weights (Fig. 7), possible punches, anvil-stones and a 'fabricator' for pressure-flaking gave an idea of the 'tool-kit'; interestingly, the valuable flakes and blades, suitable for further working, were evidently not put aside at once but left on the site to be picked out as required. Experiments have shown that striking narrow blades, which is difficult enough with good flint, requires a very high degree of skill with beach-

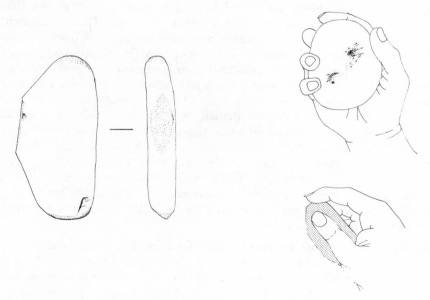

Fig. 7. Hammerstones from the Tourgis Dolmen, Alderney, in use. That on the left is shown x ½.

pebble. So the apparent simplicity of the tool-types (both in the Mesolithic and later) should not deceive us, nor should we be disappointed by the narrow range of the types. Accordingly we illustrate (Fig. 8) some artifacts of mesolithic *type,* all of which have been found in the Channel Islands, several of them among demonstrably later material.

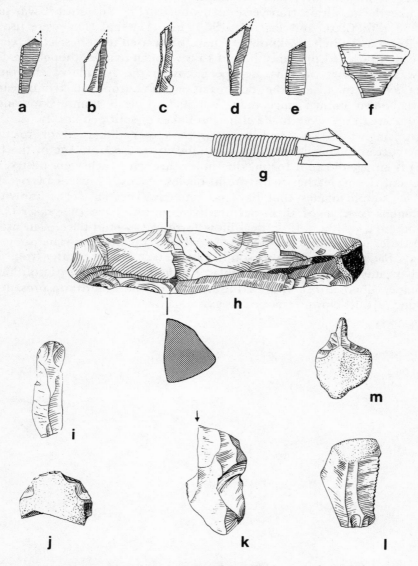

Fig. 8. Microliths and implements of mesolithic type, from Jersey and Guernsey. a-g, actual size, h-n, x ½ (sources: Hawkes 1939 for e, h, m; Kendrick 1928 for f).

The characteristic mesolithic implement is the microlith (*a–f*) of which many forms are known in Europe, hafted singly or in composite tools. In the Channel Islands we are concerned principally with microlithic arrow-heads formed from delicate narrow blades by a sophisticated notching and snapping technique. The obliquely blunted points (*a–e*) are universal forms, predominating here over the rare trapezoidal form (*f*).

17

Such trapezoidal microlithic forms are particularly numerous in European mesolithic flint assemblages dating from after about 7-6,000 B.C.—they are common forms at Téviec and Hoëdic, which can be dated close to 4,850 B.C. Their rarity in the Channel Islands may be an illusion, as our sample is too small to use with confidence. It used to be thought, incidentally, that the trapezes were set with the broad cutting edge forward, like the neolithic transverse arrow-heads (Fig. 9d) until it was suggested by Clark (1958, 26; Clark and Piggott, 1965, Fig. 41) that they were used as shown here (g). Resin and pitch are known to have been used as adhesives. A very rare tool is the so-called *pick* (h) probably bound to a wooden handle, though we do not know what it was used for; we have no specimens in the Islands of the more shapely mesolithic *axe* with which the deforestation of Europe started in earnest. Flint *scrapers* had been known since man first had to clean animal skins and use them (i, j). In our area they were made either on flakes or split pebbles. In use they become blunt surprisingly quickly, and have to be either discarded or re-chipped. The thumb- or button-scraper is found at all times up to the Iron Age in the Islands. The *borer* (m) is an age-old tool for making holes through which were passed thongs that could be cut from leather with fresh blades. Signs of use can occasionally be detected on simple blades that have no retouch. The *saw* (l) is known from only four specimens (not all of them necessarily mesolithic) and the *graver* (k) sharpened and re-sharpened with a deft vertical blow (arrowed) would have been used to groove bone and antler until splinters could be prized out. The blanks for harpoons were made in this way. Sadly, we have no mesolithic artifacts in bone or antler from the Islands—or indeed in any of the other perishable organic materials. The Mesolithic must have been a phase, albeit a lost one, in the history of the Islands; on present knowledge it passed and left little or no trace of its existence.

FARMERS AND MEGALITHS

The Mesolithic may well be an elusive phase in the history of the Islands; the presence of the succeeding *Neolithic* settlers, on the other hand, is unmistakable—both in the material equipment and in the monuments. They were, in fact, the first farmers of Europe, and it is to Central Europe and beyond, to the plains and valleys of the Danube, that we must turn for their cultural origins. We should not, however, look further to the east, as recent research on the radiocarbon dating of organic materials has exploded the older hypothesis that the neolithic way of life originated in the Near East and was 'diffused' over several millennia into northern and western Europe. This is generally expressed in terms of 'routes' by land and sea and shown as broad arrows sweeping into France and along the Mediterranean and Atlantic seaways. The truth now seems to be that evolution and transmission of techniques took place on a more regional scale. In Europe, our dates are much earlier than was formerly thought possible; so within a new framework of dates we can begin to think again about colonisation, settlement and cultural advance. It is still true to think of the Channel Islands as late in the process; and of the settlers as bringing with them the accumulated experience of generations of neolithic living.

The neolithic way of life is characterised by three important advances, the cultivation of cereals, the domestication of animals, and the introduction of pottery. The significance of the first two is clear: the change from food-gathering to food-production implies a settled way of life—at least long enough in one place to see the annual cycle completed. In some parts of the world true towns and cities are found; in Europe we must think of simple wooden houses in small, nucleated villages, their inhabitants clearing and enriching the newly-conquered land by the primitive technique of 'slash and burn'. Inevitably, primitive cultivation techniques exhausted the land, and communities would have moved on, into virgin territory; such movement from coastal settlement to pioneer occupation of inland territory has been identified at this time in Brittany (Giot, 1979, 341). For a millennium or more there was ample space, even for a rapidly expanding population; the problems started when this advance reached the 'Atlantic Façade', with only a few offshore islands to absorb the overspill. As we shall see, it is possible to suggest a different social structure for the Channel Islands and an enhancement of the individuality of the island communities.

Of the neolithic settlements in the Islands, we know disappointingly little. In several places in Jersey, Guernsey and Herm the wind has scoured the surface revealing scatters of flints, burnt material and pottery, but only excavation can confirm that these are settlement sites. One Jersey site discovered in this way, on the Blanches Banques, may have its origins in the earlier neolithic. Promising signs, moreover, of a very early settlement are appearing at Les Fouaillages, Guernsey, which is under excavation at the time of writing. One settlement, however, has been completely excavated—at

19

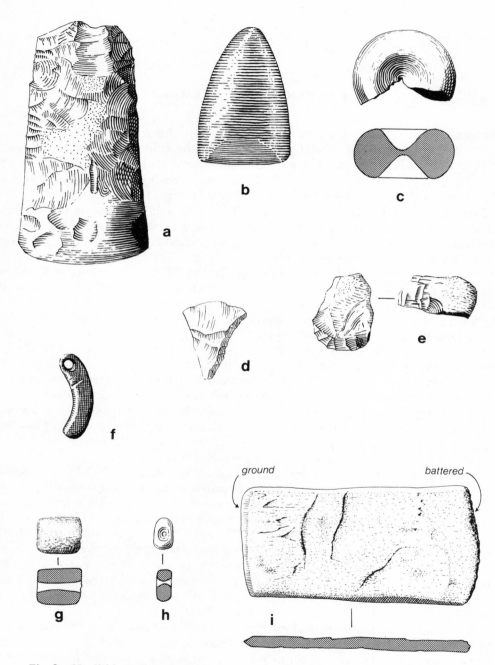

Fig. 9. Neolithic tools and adornments, all x ½ (source: Hawkes 1939 for d and f).

the base of the Pinnacle Rock, Jersey (p. 86). The excavators' account of the earliest levels is not consistent, but the hearths and rubbish-deposits seem to have preceded the first 'rampart' which was probably a retaining wall for an earthen platform at the base of the rock, supposedly for further dwellings. There was, in fact, no sign of structures, and it has been suggested (Renouf and Urry, 1976) that this was, for a while, an axe-making factory using a fine vein of dolerite that should make the products identifiable when the time comes to look for them. The polished stone *axe,* shaped by flaking and smoothed by rubbing on a coarse stone, was a major neolithic introduction. A really sharp edge was formed in this way, and it could be re-sharpened. Set in a wooden handle—often with an antler sleeve for greater resilience, it was, as experiments have demonstrated, a most effective tool for forest clearance. Set at right-angles to its handle it was an *adze,* possibly for shaping wood, but more probably for digging and hoeing. Some specimens were perforated, first by pecking with a stone tool and then by drilling with a stick and sand. The results formed *hammers* of different weights, and possibly ceremonial *mace-heads.* We should note the large number of 'unfinished mace-heads' (Fig. 9, c) which were really the hand-held top bearings for vertical wooden shafts rotated by a bow-drill and presumably used for drilling and fire-making. Other simple stone 'pounders' and 'mauls' show smooth areas suggesting that they were used as *grain-rubbers* for grinding corn or seeds on a hollowed stone base (Fig. 10). Thin chisel-like beach-pebbles (Fig. 9, i) were probably used for prising limpets from the rocks. Flint still played a part, but only for small cutting, boring and scraping tools, pendants and beads (Fig. 9, e–h) and for *transverse arrow-heads* (d) whose cutting edge faced forwards in place of the more conventional point. This form requires expert core-preparation and controlled flaking, which is doubly difficult in beach-pebble flint. This is stone technology pushed to its limits at a period when, by definition, metal was unknown.

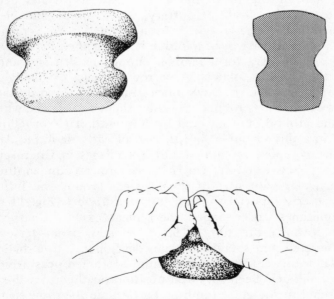

Fig. 10. Grain-rubber, Alderney, x ¼.

The polished axe is a work of art, a joy to handle and look at. We suspect that its makers thought so, too, judging from the care with which they selected rare and beautiful materials, serpentine, callaïs and jadeite. The best axes were clearly articles of prestige, kept for display rather than for everyday use. They were passed from hand to hand, frequently over immense distances. It would be wrong to think of this as 'trade' in our modern commercial sense, or even a barter in some primitive market-place. Our understanding of ancient society is based on observation of more recent primitive communities, where goods and services—and, of course, labour—are distributed equitably within the community under the supervision of a head man or chieftain. On a wider scale this would explain the distribution of everyday artifacts and raw materials, such as the distinctive, honey-coloured flint from Le Grand Pressigny in Touraine, which reached the Channel Islands in small quantities. Ceremonial gift-exchange would account for the great distances that really precious items seem to have travelled in antiquity. In the Neolithic such a social organisation would make available the vast amounts of labour required for the ambitious megalithic enterprises, principally the collective tombs, that might otherwise seem beyond the means of communities living at subsistence level.

How far the indigenous mesolithic population came to terms with the newcomers is impossible to tell from the artifacts. The pottery, however, is a good indicator of the new cultural influences. From about 4000 B.C. the Danubian people identified by their *Linear Pottery* were pushing into north-western Europe; pottery of their latest phase has been found in the Paris Basin, and is the distant ancestor of the pottery styles of Normandy, Brittany and the Channel Islands. More specifically we can parallel the decoration of the *Cerny* group in Guernsey and in Jersey (for example at The Pinnacle). The impressed decoration of dotted lines and bands, and the distinctive 'oculus' (Figs. 11 a, b) belong to the earliest settlement at The Pinnacle, in the first half of the third millennium B.C. A parallel penetration of Armorica gave birth to the *Carn* style of pottery, whose simple but elegant round-bottomed bowls were found in the so-called 'beehive hut' at La Sergenté in Jersey (Fig. 11 c). Although no burials have been found in it, this is the first true *passage-grave* in Jersey (Fig. 32, Plate 6), of a form familiar enough in Brittany and Normandy but unique so far in the Channel Islands. A narrow passage, originally roofed with large slabs, enters a small chamber that was once vaulted by the primitive technique of overlapping courses of slabs to produce a beehive-shaped roof. The whole was built on a natural rise in the ground, and covered by a mound. The corbelling technique can now be matched in a tiny chamber or *cist,* also of early neolithic date, that was an earlier phase in the complex mound at Les Fouaillages in Guernsey. Corbelled passage-graves like the Jersey example, singly or in groups, are another link with the Paris Basin, in particular with sites of the *Chasséen* group. This influence shows well in one of its characteristic pottery forms, the *vase-support* (Fig. 11 d). These are sometimes tubular, sometimes saucer-shaped; the typical 'eastern' Chassey form, with sides sloping inwards towards the top, is largely missing from Jersey where the 'western' form, with waisted and splayed profile, developed into a distinctive island form. The more tubular forms are suitable for round-bottomed pots, which have even (at La Pouquelaye de Faldouet) been found in position on them; on the other hand, all but one of those found in the great tomb of La Hougue Bie show signs of burning in their saucers, and two had been placed, like lamps or incense-burners, on either side of the entrance to the terminal chamber. The varied shapes and decoration of the Jersey specimens are eclipsed by those of Brittany, particularly the islet of Er

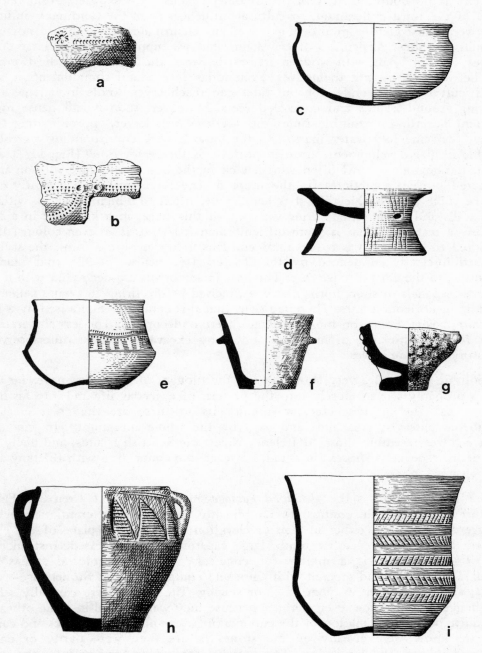

Fig. 11.   Neolithic and early Bronze Age pottery (sources: Godfray and Burdo 1949
for a and b (x ½); Hawkes 1939 for c-i (x ¼)).

23

Lannic in the Morbihan. As we shall see, the links with this part of Brittany were very strong.

There is no doubt, then, that the Channel Islands were exposed, from the early years of the third millennium, to cultural influences from the Continent—influences that were subsequently modified in an island environment. We should not under-estimate the sheer difficulties of travel, in what we suppose were still large dug-out canoes or skin boats with wooden frames, between the Islands and the Continent, and between the islands themselves. Even today inter-island communication by sea is difficult for small craft, for the tides can reach seven knots in narrow straits, eddying around islands and concealed reefs. Moreover, sudden and dense fog is a frequent hazard. In neolithic times the sea level was lower, approximating to our present extreme low water mark, and the hazards were correspondingly greater. A notable insular development, again in pottery, is the *Jersey Bowl* (Fig. 11 e). It is a small, flat-bottomed bowl often with a kick in the base, sometimes with an angular carinated profile, sometimes (in the more degenerate forms) with a gently curved outline. Like all neolithic pots it is hand-made, often to a high standard, with thin, hard walls and evenly fired; firing was not, at this stage, in a kiln, but in a simple bonfire—a technique that is more difficult than it sounds if an even colour (ranging from red to dark grey) is to be obtained. This is late neolithic form, the style and decoration clearly influenced by the *Beakers* (see below, p. 32) that mark the transition to the early Bronze Age. The best Jersey bowls are decorated with a series of vertical panels of short horizontal lines, incised before firing, in a band demarcated by dots or horizontal lines. There are signs that this could be emphasised by a filling of white mastic. Some, on the other hand, were undecorated. The less elaborate ones were for domestic use, as has been shown by excavation, while others served as accessory vessels in graves.

Neolithic man had a very short life and the thought of death was never far away. It was probably woven closely into the pattern of everyday life and into his beliefs and rituals. The most spectacular monuments to these are the great megalithic chambered passage-graves built and used by the whole community. In general the passage-graves resemble those of Ireland, Wales, the Scottish Islands, and many parts of Britain, especially Wessex; in detail, however, the connection with Brittany shows most clearly.

The typical tomb is the *V-shaped Passage-grave,* such as Le Creux ès Faïes in Guernsey (Fig. 50). In contrast to La Sergenté there is no differentiation between passage and chamber, either in plan or elevation; moreover, in place of the elegant corbelled vault of the earlier tomb, large capstones are now used. Instead of the builder's skills, this is a matter for engineers, the often colossal stones being presumably moved and erected with the same equipment as at Stonehenge—rollers, levers, sheerlegs and a wooden 'crib' or staging. The stones were carefully selected for their size and shape, even perhaps because they were special in some other way; this must be the explanation of the cup-markings, axe-polishing grooves and carvings that we know were already on the stones before they were partly or entirely obscured in their final position. The uprights are set on, or just into, the ground surface and are locked into the structure without the need for supporting 'trig' stones at the base. Gaps in the wall so formed are filled with dry-stone walling, and the whole enclosed in a large mound without a ditch but often with a stone kerb of uprights. In most cases the mound and kerb have disappeared, but the surviving traces

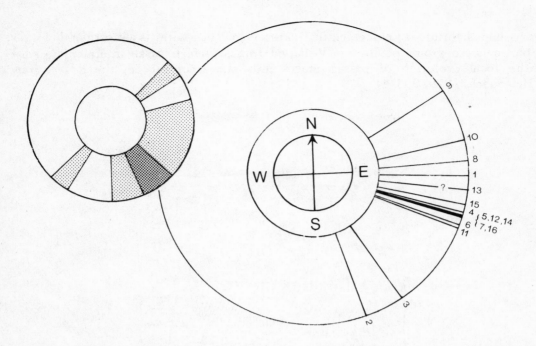

Fig. 12. Orientation of passage-graves in the Channel Islands (inset: the Armorican pattern, after L'Helgouach 1965, figs. 31-2). 1. La Hougue Bie; 2. La Sergenté; 3. Beauport; 4. Le Mont Ubé; 5. La Pouquelaye de Faldouet; 6. Les Monts Grantez; 7. Dolmen des Géonnais; 8. Le Creux ès Faies; 9. Le Trépied; 10. Le Déhus; 11. La Varde; 12. Les Pourciaux North; 13. Les Pourciaux South; 14. Herm no. 6; 15. Herm no. 12; 16. Herm no. 13.

show that they were circular. Oval or elliptical mounds are not impossible however, to judge from some Continental examples. It is reasonable, in fact, to assume that the design is an introduction from the nearer parts of France (unless we prefer to trace it further back into Central Europe and Iberia) with no particular debt to Britain or anywhere further north. Turning specifically to Brittany we find that this form is only one of many ingenious and impressive variations on the general theme developed in that Province (Giot, 1960 and 1979)—or indeed in the whole of neolithic France (Bailloud and Mieg de Boofzheim, 1955). The Breton connection is strikingly emphasised by the N.W.–S.E. orientation of the passage-graves in the Islands (Fig. 12). On the other hand, the individuality of the Channel Islands shows in one invariable difference—the rounded ends of the Channel Island examples contrast with the flat ends of the Breton ones. These tombs were intended for communal use, and therefore left open from time to time, often disturbing the remains of those already buried there, and accompanied by limpet shells, animal bones and teeth, pretty pebbles and pottery—the last not necessarily containing food for the next world as the pots were sometimes laid on their sides. As the deposits accumulated, fresh floors of beach-pebbles were laid, and the process started again; many examples of this will be found in Part 2 of this book (e.g., p. 105). Finally, when fashions changed and single burials in close *cists* became the rule, the tombs were sealed with blocking-stones and dry-stone walls at the mouths of the passages. Some, however, were left open for centuries or subsequently broken into, to judge from Iron Age and Roman pottery sherds dropped in them. They were built between 3000 and 2000 B.C., but not necessarily at the same time, as it may be possible to trace an evolution in the plans. We could follow our French colleagues' example and trace a sequence in the Channel Islands from the corbelled tomb of La Sergenté through bottle-shaped forms to Le Trépied in Guernsey (p. 102) with its almost parallel walls. In particular, a group of Breton V-shaped tombs is seen as an intermediate stage in the local evolution of passage-graves into our second type, the *gallery-grave* (L'Helgouach, 1979, 293–4).

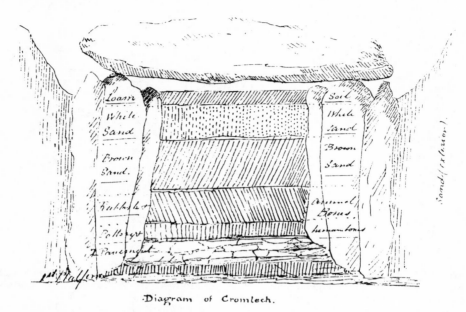

·Diagram of Cromlech.

Fig. 13. Diagram by F. C. Lukis of the stratification in a typical 'cromlech'.

The gallery-grave (sometimes known by its more attractive French name of alléé couverte) is essentially a parallel-sided cist covered by an elongated mound, often with a kerb. Some have a short 'vestibule' at one end formed not by narrowing the plan but by using one or two uprights, each with a notch at the side, to make a 'kennel-hole' entrance. Two such stones form a 'port hole'. These tombs, too, were used for collective burial, the entrances being either at the end or occasionally (in Brittany) at the side. As in some passage-graves, the floors were neatly paved. Only one true gallery-grave is known in the Islands, at Le Couperon, Jersey (p. 81). though even here the plan has been made unreliable by inaccurate restoration. For example, when the true nature of the notched slab was recognised the structure, already restored, was too narrow to receive it as an internal divider: so it was replaced at the eastern end. A second example, at Ville-ès-Nouaux, Jersey (p. 77) may have had additional structures at the eastern end, unrecognised by its excavators who thought that it was a ruined passage-grave and were expecting a chamber. The kerb on one side has survived, and seven capstones, showing that this was an exceptionally low example. A possible third, at Forest Hill, Jersey, was identified by its excavators as a gallery-grave on very slender evidence. It has now disappeared entirely. The ultimate inspiration of this form might be (according to one view) the trench-built gallery-graves of the *SOM* (Seine-Oise-Marne) group, particularly those of the Paris Basin. The SOM pottery lacks the decorative richness of the preceding Chasséen, and is typified by the simple hand-made *flower-pots* with lugs for lifting (Fig. 11 f) that are occasionally found in the Channel Islands. On the other hand, gallery-graves are plentiful in Brittany, where their inland distribution contrasts with the

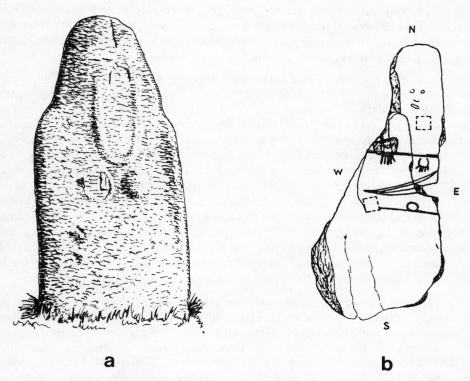

Fig. 14. Neolithic carvings in Guernsey; a) statue-menhir at Câtel; b) carvings on capstone, Déhus (drawing by T. W. M. de Guérin).

predominantly coastal pattern of the passage-graves, and where the allée couverte is recognised as a purely local development from the V-shaped passage-graves.

Two particularly striking passage-graves—one in each main island—call for special mention. The Déhus, in Guernsey (p. 103) is notable for the provision of side-chambers, of which four ar least are authentic (two date from the disastrous 're-excavation' and restoration of 1933), and for the carving on the underside of the capstone (Fig. 14 b). This faint and enigmatic figure (known as the 'guardian of the tomb' since its discovery in 1917) has been variously interpreted as a goddess, a bearded Hermes and a male archer; a determined attempt was made by De Guérin (1919) and Kendrick (1928, 29–33) to link it—albeit distantly—to representations of the human figure in southern France, Portugal and elsewhere. On the analogy of the statue-menhirs it is usually taken to be female, though there is absolutely no sign of breasts—and a beard has even seen on some of the many photographs taken of it (e.g., Collum, 1944, Plate IIIa, Cox, 1976, 29); the face and hands are clear enough, and so is the straight line with circle, at the base, resembling a 'baldrick'. The bow-shaped arrangement of arcs is distinctly carved, though it is difficult to identify it with the U-shaped 'collar' or 'necklace' of the statue-menhirs. If it is a bow, as in clearer representations in Finistère and the Morhiban, then we have a link with Phase 1 of Breton megalithic art (Twohig, 1977, 177). The identity of the whole composition, however, must remain speculative until other similar representations are found. The other outstanding tomb is La Hougue Bie, Jersey (p. 64) where side chambers are arranged in a neat cruciform plan. For sheer size it is unrivalled in the Islands, and its plan and craftsmanship invite comparison with the cruciform passage-graves of Ireland and Scotland, these, however, have a central corbelled vault, and the use of capstones at La Hougue Bie places it with the less impressive Breton examples. It should be thought of as an evolved form, and its significance is discussed below.

The small terminal chambers at La Hougue Bie and at Beauport (p. 71) and the single side-chamber at Les Monts Grantez, Jersey (p. 85) look like local experiments; it is acknowledged that the later fourth and third millenia were marked by independent regional variations on common architectural ideas, and the particular conditions of the Channel Islands may well have encouraged their insularity. For example, the internal compartmentation of Le Mont Ubé, Jersey (p. 73) may be an instance of an insular tendency that shows in some of the segmented cists on L'Ancresse Common, Guernsey (p. 107) and most strikingly in the miniature compartments of Les Pourciaux North, Alderney (Plate 11). Burial peculiarities include two kneeling skeletons at the Déhus and one sitting at Les Monts Grantez; the alleged burial of horse and man together at La Hougue Boëte, Jersey (p. 77) aroused speculation over possible Breton connections until the horse teeth, at least, were discovered to be modern. The unique structure at Robert's Cross, Herm (p. 116) may be a variant gallery-grave, reminiscent of the much larger 'dolmens à portique' of Anjou and the Loires.

The only possible island 'type' is represented by two Jersey tombs. The first, discovered on the Mont de la Ville in St. Helier in 1785, was presented by the grateful townspeople to the then Governor, General Conway, who had it transported to England and re-erected in his grounds at Park Place, Henley, where it now stands (Plate 9). The site is now occupied by the Recreation Centre of Fort Regent, St. Helier. Hawkes (1939, 243-4) discusses the considerable discrepancies among our sources and with the re-erected structure as to its exact form, but it seems to have been a parallel-sided passage with four or six capstones and an exactly circular 'chamber' with five internal chambers known out of a possible ten. No significant finds at all are recorded. A surrounding 'wall' is recorded (no doubt a dry-stone revetment) and the whole was covered by 'a large barrow or tumulus'. Now the large central space, over 6m. in diameter, is too large to have been roofed by capstones; moreover, our sources mention neither capstones nor the immense amount of rubble that a collapsed vault would have created. So, if our sources are to be believed, the fine covered passage led simply to a solid mound. Alternatively, we might suppose an internal wooden chamber whose traces were not recognised at the time; wooden structures have indeed been found in earthen long barrows. The combination with fine megalithic construction, however, would be noteworthy. The second example of this 'type' is the first phase at La Pouquelaye de Faldouet, also in Jersey (p. 81) though extensive reconstruction has introduced considerable uncertainties.

Our uncertainties and likely misunderstandings of what we already have are quite considerable. The possible combination of megalithic with (unrecognised) timber construction is one example. Another is the assumption that all our lost mounds were circular—they may have been wedge-shaped or oval, or may not even have existed at all in some cases. Finally, the possibility that two or more cists and circles were covered by a single mound may help us to understand grouped cists, such as the pair discovered on the beach in Guernsey in 1916 near Rousse Tower (fig. 15). Only the excavation of a fresh site can help us in these respects.

Such an opportunity has been provided by the newly-discovered site at Les Fouaillages, Guernsey, that is being excavated by the Société Guernesiaise at the

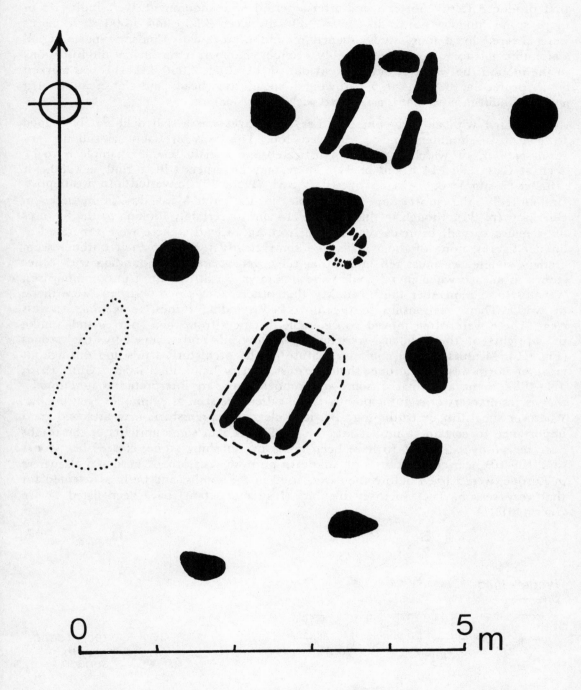

Fig. 15. Paired cists near Rousse Tower, Guernsey (source: Kendrick 1928).

time of writing. The finds are on display in the Guernsey Museum, with a provisional sequence of phases which is briefly this: upon a settlement site of about 4,000 B.C. that produced Cerny pottery, and after a period of abandonment, were built two or more stone funerary cairns in about 3,800. Between 3,500 and 3,000 these cairns were covered by a long, wedge-shaped mound of turf with Chassey-type material, a monumental stone façade and possibly a timber chamber. After further modifications to the mound the whole structure went out of use about 2,000 B.C.; this was marked by a spectacular deposit of 5 barbed-and-tanged arrowheads and the creation of a new, turf-built mound that is associated with Beaker material.

Associated with an early phase at Les Fouaillages was a slab deliberately shaped to give two shoulders and a rounded top. This was probably a rudimentary *statue-menhir,* of which a more sophisticated and overtly female example is to be seen at Catel (Fig. 14 a and p. 94). There may be others still to find; in 1980, for instance, a simple one was discovered in Sark (Plate 20) converted into a gate-post. Undoubtedly the most famous example is La Gran'-Mére du Chimquière, in Guernsey (p. 96), though in this case we are almost certainly looking at the features of a figure carved, or re-carved, in the Iron Age. Clearly, these were venerated as human figures, none of them male, and some clearly female; if their outlines seem crudely simple, we must remember that they were shaped by pounding with other stones in an age when metal tools were unknown (or at least, not in common use). We must also remember the possibility that others, long since perished, were made of wood. Their relationship to the unworked standing stones, or *menhirs,* is less clear. These were often moved considerable distances from their sources and—unlike the uprights of the dolmens—were set in shallow pits and steadied by 'trig' stones (Fig. 16). Menhirs were a common feature of the prehistoric landscape throughout most of north-western Europe, their greatest density being in Brittany (Giot, 1979, 383–408). Some are isolated, some are grouped; some are interpreted as functional— that is, as markers or sighting-points—while others are seen as symbolic, even phallic. Whatever the truth or truths may be, it is clear that prehistoric man attached great importance to certain stones; it may be significant that some uprights of the tombs bear the grooves thought to have been made by polishing stone axes. Other stones (pp. 109-10) bear cup-markings of unknown purpose. Yet others, here and elsewhere in Europe, were carved before they were used in the tombs, and perhaps selected for that very reason. The Guernsey menhirs (lost and extant) have been listed by De Guérin (1921).

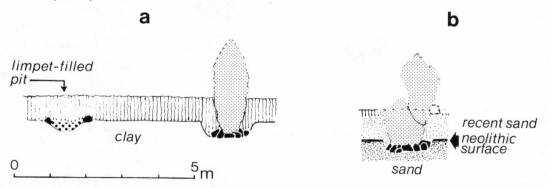

Fig. 16.   Sections through two Jersey menhirs showing the use of 'trig' stones. a) La Dame Blanche; b) The Broken Menhir (source: Rybot 1933).

From the inscrutable mysteries of neolithic religion we turn finally to the nature of neolithic society, as illuminated by the recent analysis of the passage-graves (Johnston forthcoming). Allowing for losses (which seem to be roughly uniform) the average 'burial capacity' of Jersey and Guernsey is the same, in spite of the disparity of size, while the other islands exhibit peculiarities that bear no relation to their size. In other words, we can detect no hierarchy in the islands. The same is true, at least in the early phase, of the monuments themselves. It follows that this is so of the communities that built them; for the pattern in Jersey matches that noted elsewhere (e.g., Renfrew, 1973, 132 ff) where each tomb apparently served as the focal point of a community and its territory. A special feature, however, of the Channel Islands is the varied and distinctive geology; and from petrological studies in Jersey by Dr. A. E. Mourant (1933, 1963, 1977, and elsewhere) it can be shown that the quest for stone by the builders respected the suggested territorial boundaries quite closely. This pattern of apparently autonomous communities fits the pattern of a 'segmentary' society that has been independently proposed for the whole of the Atlantic Façade (Renfrew, 1976). La Hougue Bie, however (which on other grounds can be shown to be a late creation), seems, in its souces of stone, to override the boundaries observed by its predecessors. This suggests an emerging hierarchy in Jersey, perhaps paralleled in Guernsey and Alderney, and evidenced by the obsolescence of the autonomous territories and the creation of at least one monumental 'central place'. This ambitious hypothesis, for which the supporting evidence is considerable, varies from the pattern proposed for Brittany (above, p. 19), and is merely one of several analyses in each of which the results are slightly different. Such models may well be discarded or modified by subsequent research; but they demonstrate that our interest is shifting away from the artifacts and tombs as ends in themselves to their significance as possible indicators of the nature of prehistoric society.

METAL TECHNOLOGY

The first metal artifacts to be seen in the Channel Islands, at the beginning of the third millenium B.C., will have been of copper. The newcomers were metal-users, rather than metal-workers, familiar with and using the results of a technology evolved some five centuries or so earlier in central Europe. These earlier European *chalcolithic* cultures (of which the Vinča group is the best known) were basically neolithic in spirit and material equipment, but with prestige copper objects produced by the new techniques of smelting, melting and casting. In north-western Europe the influence of metal tools is seen in the changed shape of everyday flint axes; the slight flaring of the cutting edge of Fig. 9 a, for instance, is copied from metal axes where the cast edge was sharpened and annealed by hammering before being whetted to a find edge. Copper artifacts are rare in the Channel Islands, but two flat axes are known from Jersey (The Pinnacle and La Moye) and a small tanged knife or dagger from the Déhus in Guernsey. Before long the use of bronze, a tougher alloy of copper and tin, had swept across Europe and by the middle of the third millennium, the Bronze Age proper, bronze-smiths were working in the Channel Islands. The products are among the most sophisticated and artistic objects found in the Islands, and include the great gold torque (Plate 33) from Jersey.

The phase of overlap, or transition, is characterised by pottery *beakers*—vessels that are not only ceramic masterpieces but were prestige objects with an important funerary role. Their symbolism can only be guessed: it is not merely that of provisions for the next world (for some, laid on their sides, were clearly empty). They were designed for a special drink, possibly alcoholic and ale-like (to judge from millet grains in one Portuguese example), conceivably the prerogative of a ruling caste and clearly—when considered with the daggers, battle-axes and prestige accroutements—indicating power and authority.

The finest Channel Islands examples belong to the family of the classic European Bell-Beakers and all show the characteristic S-profile. Some are plain, others decorated in horizontal zones of impressed decoration (Fig. 11) that show chronological and regional variations. The complex movements of the Beaker peoples are still disputed, but are a fine example of culture-diffusion on a local, European, scale: movements of flux and reflux, overland and maritime colonisation. The origin of much of the decoration is to be found in the earlier Corded Wares of central Europe and beyond, and in peoples whose practice of single burial was a break with the neolithic communal tombs; it is interesting, therefore, to note that in Brittany and the Channel Islands the communal passage-graves continued to be used, being our principal source of the beakers. British readers, of course, will be familiar with the crouched Beaker burials in round barrows: these are the counterpart of the later cists of the Channel Islands. If this continued use of the passage-graves implies a time-lag, we should remember one of the phenomena of colonisation demonstrated by Case (1969, 182–183), that of 'a stable period of adjustment' before a community's efforts can be re-directed from subsistence and warfare to the building of monuments.

The Jersey bowls (or at least, the later ones) belong to this phase of transition, as do the beakers. One further little pot (Fig. 11, g) belongs to this phase. It is of coarse, gritty fabric and stands a mere 7mm. high; the solid foot has four deep holes made, apparently, by poking a small finger into the clay. The four rows of knobs are applied and roughly smoothed down. In Brittany, the tradition of applied knobs to pottery goes back to the full megalithic phases of the fourth millennium; on the other hand, this one bears an important resemblance to the 'grape cups' of Wessex—miniature accessory vessels with bronze daggers accompanying single inhumations of about 1800 B.C. Nothing else like it is known from the Channel Isles.

Before we turn to the bronze artifacts, let us follow the pottery series through the Bronze Age. Fig. 11 h shows a particularly spectacular type of vessel, of which ten or more examples have been found on six separate sites in Jersey (but none in Guernsey). All are presumed to have had four ribbon-handles, as is usually the case in Brittany; for this is a characteristic Armorican form, often with quite elaborate and tasteful decoration of chevrons, triangles and even imitation basket-work. The number of handles can range from one to four. Sherds of several have come from settlements in Jersey (La Pulente, Petit Port, St. Helier, and The Pinnacle), and one, unstratified, from Ville-ès-Nouaux. Three were found in the passage-grave of Mont-Ubé, indicating the continued use of this tomb well into the Bronze Age. But most significantly one is recorded from the destroyed structure at Les Hougues de Millais. This—as far as the scanty records indicate—represents a new form of tomb, a long cist walled with dry-stone but still megalithic in its large covering slabs. This may have still been for collective burial, but a thick layer of ashes is recorded, suggesting cremation. This corresponds well with the Breton tumuli, especially those of Finistère, which usually contain rather smaller funerary pits with dry-stone walls and large capstones. They contained either cremations or single inhumations, seemingly of princely status and accompanied by ribbon-handled urns, daggers, etc. They belong to the early and middle Bronze Age, and one recently has been given a date of c. 1800 B.C. They show the decline of the megalithic tradition and introduce the practice of single burial.

On the whole, the Bronze Age pottery of the Channel Islands and Brittany is otherwise rather undistinguished. Shapes are clumsy and irregular (still, of course, hand-made) and decoration is limited to cordons, lugs and knobs. Some are large and barrel-shaped, others rather resemble buckets. An easily identified form is the smaller 'flower-pot' which often has lugs for handles. One such was found in a structure at Les Platons, Jersey, resembling that at Les Hougues de Millais, this time a mound 8.2m. in diameter encircled by stones with a central dry-stone cist. There were two pots here—a bucket-urn packed with cremations and a smaller 'flower-pot' beside it, empty (Fig. 47). In another large Jersey tumulus, La Hougue Mauger, six empty 'flower-pots' were set in a semi-circle around a central cist that was destroyed before it could be examined. The Breton connection here is very strong, and can be paralleled, for instance, in the recent excavation of le Tumulus de Ligollenec in Berien, near Huelgoat (Briard, 1977) with its date of 1550±130 B.C. But the idea has its roots in central Europe and the movements of the Urnfield people. Two further Jersey sites probably belong to this phase—Les Cinq Pierres (now destroyed, but containing an inhumation) and the badly wrecked Hougue de Vinde (p. 72); these five tumuli with their cists, urns and stone ring-walls apparently show a fusion of native and more distant traditions.

The megalithic tradition really ends in the Bronze Age with the cists in mounds, often—but not always—with stone kerbs. These have suffered more than most at the hands of quarrymen and tomb-robbers, so that our knowledge of their contents is extremely scanty. It is particularly disappointing that the two most recently excavated —those of Tourgis, in Alderney, and Clouet Bay in Sark—both failed to produce burial goods for close dating. The Alderney example was a neatly-built cist of four slabs, whereas the Clouet Bay structure and its neighbour at La Vermandée (pp. 121-4) both show an economy of effort and lack of sophistication that must place them at the end of the series. On the other hand, the tradition of cist-burial continued vigorously well into the Iron Age.

The bronze artifacts show clearly how the Channel Islands were in the mainstream of the new European technology. Metallurgy, however, is probably a symptom rather than a cause of the changes taking place in society (as we understand it) in about 2000 B.C. Neolithic society had developed a structure in which the chieftain directed the re-distribution of goods, services and manpower; a limited degree of specialisation could be seen, for instance in the manufacture of implements at The Pinnacle, Jersey. Our understanding is that in the Bronze Age society became more stratified, more specialised; and that the emphasis was less on the mobilisation of manpower for public works and more on the display of personal prestige and authority. So we can see a warrior aristocracy and a body of specialised bronze-founders working for them. The former sometimes hoarded their wealth; and the deposit of 88 socketed axes found in St. Helier in 1836, of which two-thirds were miniatures of Breton type, must represent a practice well known on both sides of the Channel. But the other hoards, in Jersey and Alderney, are different. They comprise up to 200 pieces, and belong to the later Bronze Age when the metal was more plentiful and the 9:1 ratio of copper to tin was being modified with the occasional admixture of lead.

Some implements are worn-out or obsolete, and many have been deliberately broken into small pieces for the melting-pot. Occasionally metal-working tools and cakes of raw bronze are also found. The conventional interpretation is that these represent the stock-in-trade and raw materials of itinerant founders, collecting scrap and making up-to-date objects on the spot for a while, and burying the materials in readiness for a return visit. The international character of this activity is shown by the objects themselves: detailed study is now beginning to identify precise sources for some objects, such as the *socketed axe* with the distinctive double ring at the top from the latest Jersey hoard, a type which was probably made in the Cotentin or Ile-et-Vilaine and was seldom exported. A broad-bladed spearhead with lunate openings in the blade, from the same hoard, is also typically Breton. So, too, are two pegged leaf-shaped spearheads in Jersey and Guernsey; and the famous Jersey Torque, in gold, is an import from Brittany. The same Jersey hoard and the Alderney hoard both contain a specifically Wessex type of socketed spearhead (Fig. 17 g), while from Alderney comes a rare barbed spearhead that is the distinguishing mark of the Broadward group in the west of England. The Jersey hoard also contains examples of swords of the Wilburton group, distinguished by their heavy leaf-shaped blades. Finally, we should mention the bronze *dress-fastener* (Fig. 17 e) from La Rocque Qui Sonne, Guernsey, a type that is familiar (in gold) from Ireland, and the *belt-fastener* of Fig. 17 d that is a masterpiece of bronze technology.

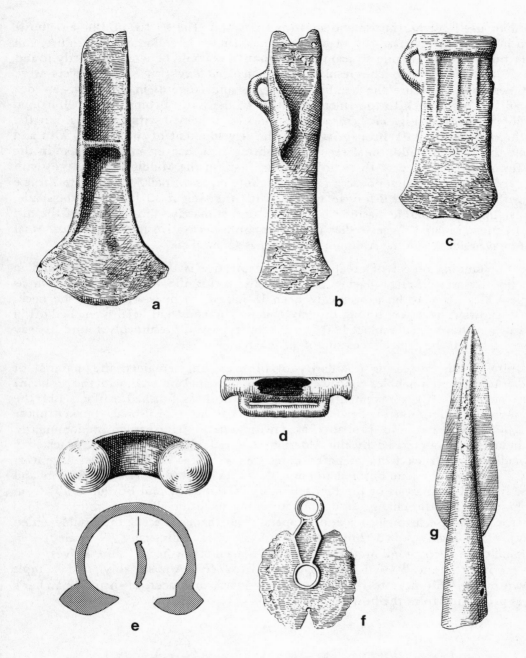

Fig. 17.   Bronze artifacts from Jersey, Guernsey and Alderney, x ½
(sources: Hawkes 1939 for a, Kendrick 1928 for d and e).

A good sequence of implements in the museums of Jersey, Guernsey and Alderney
show the evolution of casting techniques from flat axes cast in open moulds to the use
of multiple moulds with plugs inserted to form the sockets. The *palstave* (Fig. 17a) has
pockets on both faces to receive a split haft, and a stop-ridge to prevent the head

embedding itself further in use and splitting the wood. The haft would be an elbow-shaped handle. Side-flanges, cast or hammered, restricted lateral movement in use, and in time these flanges became so pronounced that they could be wrapped partly round the haft by hammering. The result was the *winged axe* (Fig. 17b). Rivets were sometimes used to secure the handles of *daggers* and *halberds* in particular—an idea that can be traced back to the Unetice culture of the Early Bronze Age in Bohemia. Basal loops on *axes* (Fig. 17c), *spearheads* and *sickles* helped with fastening, but the breakthrough in the later Bronze Age was the development of the socket—with and without the loop for additional security. Fighting with dagger and battle-axe in the early Bronze Age gave way to sword-fighting, first (in the Middle Bronze Age) with long, narrow *rapiers* that suppose a fencing technique, and finally (in the late Bronze Age) with the elegant *carps-tongue swords*. With the weight so far down the blade, we must imagine a heroic slashing technique; unfortunately, the fragility of the hilt (with frequent repairs) suggests that they were more decorative than functional. Most seem to have ended, like the Alderney example, as scrap.

The outstanding object of great beauty and prestige is the gold *torque* found in St. Helier by a workman digging the foundations for the houses now known as 'Torque Villas'. It may have originally been U-shaped, to be worn round the neck; Plate 33 shows it as it was found, crudely coiled. The ends had been wrenched off in antiquity and have been replaced. It is a Breton type and presumably found its way to Jersey through the princely custom of gift-exchange.

In spite of the increasing popularity of bronze, flint remained the material of everyday tools. Beach-pebbles continued to be the principal material, with the problems already noted (p. 16), supplemented by imports—both as finished artifacts like the highly-wrought Breton arrow-heads that belong to the transitional, Beaker phase of *c.*2,000 B.C., and also probably as raw materials. The earlier predominantly flake industry, characterised by the Alderney material, changes to one in which long thin blades were struck from prepared cores. Small blades could be used as gravers (but still without the true burin sharpening-flake), as 'planes', borers, fabricators and strike-a-lights. The analysis of the Pinnacle material (Godfray and Burdo, 1950) from this phase shows little change from the preceding neolithic. Beach-pebbles provided flakes for transverse arrow-heads and scrapers of all shapes (except the double-ended variety). The highly-prized brown flint of Le Grand-Pressigny (Touraine) can occasionally be recognised in the barbed-and-tanged arrow-heads, flint knives, etc., that were imitated locally with varying degrees of success. A reasonably good example is shown in Fig. 18b; next to it is a stone wrist-guard, or bracer, sewn to the archer's glove as protection from the bowstring.

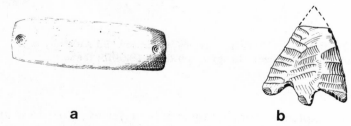

a   **b**

Fig. 18.   Neolithic and Bronze Age archery: a) stone wrist-guard x ½; b) barbed and tanged arrow-head, actual size
(source: Hawkes 1939)

Numerous working-floors or areas in the Islands can probably be ascribed to the Bronze Age, and doubtless some of the shell-middens, though they all lack diagnostic artifacts. In the absence of pottery, hearths and structures, they can hardly be called permanent settlements; evidence for the last is still elusive. However, finds in the south-west corner of Jersey, and especially in the Quennevais dunes of St. Ouen's Bay that are known as Les Blanches Banques, demonstrate the warm, dry climate of the period. Layers of blown sand sealing at least one ground surface with worked flints (and on one occasion a substantial post-hole) can occasionally be recognised in the sand-pits. The suddenness of these prehistoric sand-storms was revealed in 1918, in an area that had been used as a prisoner-of-war camp, when a storm exposed the prehistoric land-surface and its evidence of occupation; a Bronze Age pot was found, upright and filled with limpet-shells, overwhelmed by the blown sand. In 1976, fieldwork located the most important site of all a few hundred metres to the south, where wind-erosion and human feet had exposed a concentration of pottery and flints. Two seasons' excavation so far has confirmed that this horizon is contemporary with the nearby 'Ossuary' with its collective burials. Moreover, the elusive structures have appeared at last—numerous stake-holes, probably supporting wickerwork windbreaks or even more substantial structures. There is an extensive flaking area, and another for pot-making and -firing, with four clay hearths and polishing-tools. The flint industry is typical of the transition from neolithic to Bronze Age, with flake scrapers and small blades and a good array of fabricators, hammer- and anvil-stones. The pottery includes sherds of a late, degraded form of Jersey Bowl. A radiocarbon date suggests *c.* 2300 B.C. (though this is not from a sealed deposit).

Ribbon-handled sherds of an Armorican Bronze Age pot are the clue to a later settlement still to be found below the hill in St. Helier, but for occupation of the later Bronze Age we turn to the confused Phase II at The Pinnacle (p. 86) when the outermost 'rampart' was added. This, however, may not have been a true settlement. A date for this phase is suggested by the bronze spearhead found outside the enclosure. The combination of pegged socket and basal loops places it in the Pennard phase at the beginning of the late Bronze Age.

In the Channel Islands the Bronze Age seems to merge imperceptibly into the Iron Age. The first sign of the influence of the iron-using Hallstatt people of Austria comes from the only true late Bronze Age urnfield in the Channel Islands, found outside the megalithic structures at Ville-ès-Nouaux, Jersey. Several of these cinerary urns have been restored (not entirely accurately) and the most convincing is shown in Fig. 19. These jars are actually imitations in pottery of the typical Hallstatt *situla* or bucket of sheet bronze, of which examples—clearly much prized and admired—were finding their way across the Channel by about 600 B.C. During the seventh century the new technology of iron-working had been introduced into Europe, and the first iron objects are now found alongside the current bronze forms; significantly, the first to reach the Channel Islands (as elsewhere) were swords. It was a century or so before iron became the material for tools of everyday use throughout Europe, owing to the ubiquity and relative cheapness of the ores; apparently it took even longer in the Islands, where there are no native ores at all. But the new iron technology brought about the abandonment of the established designs of tools and weapons, for purely technical reasons. These bronze designs were dictated by the technique of casting, whereas iron had to be forged: primitive furnaces could not reach the temperature for melting iron. The lack of ironwork from this phase in the Islands is not merely

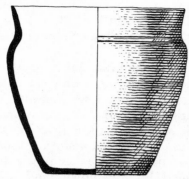

Fig. 19. Urn from the urnfield,
Ville-ès Nouaux, Jersey (source:
Hawkes 1939)

because this metal survives badly in acid, granitic conditions; it reminds us that bronze continued to be used for many everyday objects, such as buckets, and for personal adornments, such as the brooches (Fig. 21).

A few unrecognisably corroded iron objects from The Pinnacle show that occupation continued for a while here; the pottery, however, is still Bronze Age in character, emphasising the ceramic conservatism of the Islands in the seventh and sixth centuries B.C. Nevertheless, the wind of ceramic change was blowing across the Channel from the vigorous La Tène developments on the Continent. Pottery forms from Jersey and Alderney (Plate 34) would be familiar both in France and in southern Britain. But the use of the potter's wheel, which could produce exciting new shapes such as those in Fig. 23, established itself very gradually. For we still see hand-made wares of Late Bronze Age type being made in Alderney on a site (p. 00) that must be unique in Iron Age Europe—a settlement and a pot-making factory combined. The bronze razor (Fig. 17f) is a recognisably Bronze Age type, but the pottery, although hand-made, shows an advanced skill in both form and finish (Plate 34), while a group of attractive pottery spindle-whorls is shown in Fig. 20. The dry-stone enclosure at

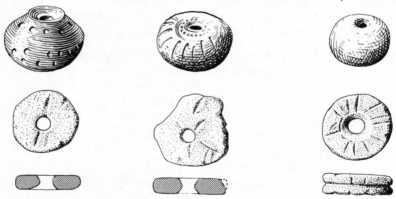

Fig. 20. Spindle-whorls, probably of the Iron Age, x ½. Top: pottery specimens from Alderney; below: 'rouettes de faïtiaux' (fairy rings) in stone, from Sark.

Les Huguettes was evidently the focus of a village, and was accompanied, at the nearby Kennels site, by a substantial stone-built structure of quite unknown purpose. Even so, there is no hint here of the social, religious and artistic developments elsewhere that were transforming Europe and southern Britain into what we recognise as the flowering of the Celtic world.

THE LATER IRON AGE

Warfare is something we readily associate with the Celtic world: and, indeed, throughout France and southern Britain the last generations before the coming of Rome saw the climax of the hill-forts—the refuges and castles of the later Iron Age. The fortifications of the Channel Islands are not, on the whole, true hill-forts, but rather promontory-forts of the kind that Caesar found in Armorica. In these, the human effort is concentrated into multiple defences across the neck of a promontory, leaving nature to look after the rest. In the case of the Veneti the landward defences were supplemented by an effective fleet. The smaller islands, Alderney (p. 133) and Sark (p. 125) each seem to have had one, though the existing traces are far from certain. These would have been partly demonstrations of chieftainly prestige, partly admissions of the vulnerability of islands in an age of determined seamanship. Jersey was large enough to boast at least four, probably more. That at Frémont (pp. 78-9) was a relatively simple affair, a single bank with a ditch facing inland, the excavations were admittedly incomplete, but no sign was found of the often very sophisticated timber framework, rampart-facing and palisade that the Gaulish examples display. The finest Jersey example, at Le Câtel (pp. 91-2), still awaits proper investigation, and even its date is uncertain. But enough finds of both the later Iron Age and the Roman period show that it had a long life. Within the defences will have been a settlement, but only extensive excavation could tell us whether this was permanent or temporary and intermittent. The most magnificent promontory-fort of all is at Jerbourg, Guernsey (p. 95), even in its present mutilated condition. The three ramparts are not necessarily contemporary; at the time of writing only the uppermost has been sectioned with a single trench, and interpretations of this are provisional. Much of its present form is now known to be the result of medieval remodelling, but it is basically an Iron Age work of turf (possibly stone-faced for a time) immediately above a deep ditch. There was little or no berm, so the combined slope of ditch and bank must have been considerable. This glacis-style defence, presenting a unified slope to an attacker, was easier to maintain than the earlier stone- or timber-fronted types of rampart and avoided the problem of rebuilding the vertical face when undermined by erosion. At Jerbourg there is a smaller primary rampart embedded in the later work and well to the rear or it. This is undated, and might even go back to the later Bronze Age. A clue to the settlement that lay behind it is the discovery of typical Iron Age triangular loom-weights of clay and spinning-whorls.

To find the burial-places of the class presumably responsible for these cliff-castles we must turn to Guernsey, and to a remarkable series of over thirty stone-built cists that were found in the western part of the island during the 19th century and the early part of the 20th century. Sometimes single, sometimes grouped, each cist resembled a miniature gallery-grave (Plate 13) and was little more than two metres long—sufficient, in fact, for a single extended inhumation with grave-goods. In common with La Tène burials in Gaul and Britain these graves were lavishly furnished with fine, wheel-made pots (local and imported, e.g., Fig. 23), bronze objects, and—most importantly—iron knives, swords in scabbards, and spears. The bones had perished leaving only the weapons to indicate the sex of the occupants. The sickle found in one, however, might indicate a female, and an unusual combination at La Hougue au Comte of weapons, bronze finger-rings and beads of jet, amber and glass could belong to a rare double burial. Acid soil conditions had seriously corroded the ironwork, but current conservation treatment at Oxford is revealing, on one sword from Richmond, evidence for a strap, a wooden handle and a diagonal bandage with which it was wrapped—a La Tène practice known in Germany and elsewhere. Interestingly, the burial rite was inhumation, as in contemporary Breton burials, in contrast to the trend towards cremation which was becoming normal elsewhere. At present these warrior burials are confined to one part of one island, and not securely related to settlements. It is possible, however, that the recently-excavated enclosure at Kings Road, St. Peter Port (p. 43) may help to fill this gap in our knowledge.

The glass beads from La Hougue au Comte are large and gaily coloured: one is marbled blue and yellow, another is streaked with white and yellow, while a third, unperforated, is a curved drop of amethyst glass. Two in Jersey are of pale greenish-grey glass, one with indigo-hued spiral ribbing, the other with a band and loop motif in black and Indian red. A third Jersey specimen—a chance find like the others—is dark brown with crackled and pitted rings in greenish white (Fig. 21), resembling a rhyolite pebble (which is how it was first accessioned in the museum). 'We may', commented Hawkes (1939, 112), 'safely picture these gay baubles adding to the barbaric splendour of some Gaul of the 1st century B.C.'.

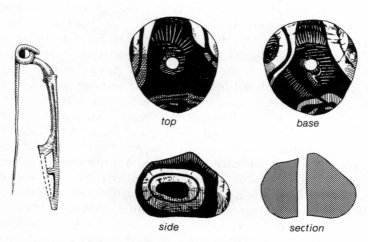

top   base

side   section

Fig. 21. Celtic finery, from Jersey. Left: bronze brooch, x ½;
right: glass bead x 1 (source for the bead: Hawkes 1939).

Bronze *fibulae*, or brooches, were another important element in late La Tène finery and played a part in the interchange of luxury goods across the Channel. Unfortunately there are no examples now in the Islands, the only three (e.g., Fig. 21) having been stolen from the Jersey Museum. Although broken, they were typical La Tène forms,

40

working on the safety-pin principle with a coiled spring and a pin engaging in a perforated, triangular catch-plate. They were worn both by men and women. The type has an Iron Age Mediterranean ancestry and became universal throughout the Roman world sometimes in simple, sometimes in grotesquely elaborated designs. The scanty Channel Islands material barely enables us to visualise the colourful splendour of these people who so impressed the writers of the classical world, though the coin obverses (Fig. 22) offer an authentic glimpse of an idealised barbarism. In this connection we should consider what must be an important piece of Celtic sculpture, the statue-menhir in Guernsey known as the Gran'-Mère du Chimquière (Plate 19 and p. 96), probably a neolithic statue remodelled in Celtic or early Roman times. Here, as in the coin, are the solemn, lentoid eyes; these eyes, nose and mouth are the hallmark of sculptured heads throughout Europe. There are very few such 'Celtic Heads' in the Islands, and none in a public collection. But they remind us of a less attractive aspect of Celtic life and religion, the cult of the (severed) head.

Fig. 22.   Armorican coin from Jersey (drawing by N. L. V. Rybot).

It is the coins that bring home to us that by the first century B.C. England had entered the historic period and was feeling the influence of the classical world. These silver-alloy coins, minted in Armorica and deposited by the thousand in hoards in the second half of the first century, represent not only a new and vigorous art form but also a sign that commercial, as well as cultural contacts required the creation of a native currency on the classical model. Even the coin-type has classical origins—the gold stater of Philip II of Macedon for this particular series, though coins of Alexander and others served elsewhere for models. The reverse of the Philippic stater showed a two-horse chariot and driver that was evidently copied, copied again and misunderstood many times in its course of transformation at the hands of native die-cutters. The Channel Islands series was minted in the Gaulish tribe of the Coriosolites of northern and central Britanny; by now the orthodox Macedonian original had completed its metamorphosis into something wild and exciting that is—to many eyes—artistically preferable to its original. The single horse is almost a symbol of a major Celtic preoccupation, while the chariot has become a boar with a circle beneath it and the feathered 'whisk' above it is thought by some to be not the driver but a winged victory derived ultimately from a Syracusan type. The first serious study of these was a classic paper in 1937 by N. L. V. Rybot, later revised (1952). The complicated task of analysis has been continued by Dr. J. B. Colbert de Beaulieu and others to the present day. The diagrammatic coin-profiles of the Jersey hoards are comparable to those of the French hoards, and one in particular resembles that from le Petit Celland which we know was buried in 56 B.C. In that year Caesar put down a rebellion by the Veneti of Brittany, destroying the navy and enslaving much of the population. Coin-hoards are often understood to be a panic reaction to crisis: is this, perhaps, reflected in the Jersey hoards? In fact, the inclusion of a few Roman Republican and even Augustan issues still circulating 50 years later suggests a movement of wealth from Gaul to the Islands and a rather later deposition of some hoards at least. But the old hypothesis that these were the savings of refugees from Roman Gaul may still be valid, reflecting the subsequent troubles at home a generation or more after the Roman conquest.

This explanation might suit the most remarkable hoard of all, discovered in Sark in 1739 and now lost. Detailed drawings (intended, apparently, for engraving, but not published) came to light recently and have been published by D. F. Allen (1971). An iron-bound pottery urn contained 18 Gaulish and Roman Republican coins, dating the hoard to about 30–20 B.C. In addition there were 13 highly ornamented gilded silver discs (Plate 35) and an elaborate mounting, presumably from a saddle. The discs, too, are horse-trappings, or *phalerae,* whose decoration is neither classical nor truly Celtic. They can probably be traced to Thrace (roughly modern Bulgaria) whose horsemen were much in demand as mercenary cavalry both in Celtic Europe and, rather later, as auxiliary units of the Roman army. Precisely how these items came to Sark is quite uncertain, but in general they must point to continued, and unrecorded, unrest in Gaul during the early years of Augustus' rule.

Augustus's efforts to Romanise Gaul come at the end of two centuries of Roman exploitation of Gaul and Spain. Armorica, the Channel Islands and Britain were now engaging in 'trade' in something approaching its modern meaning. Money will not have played a great part in it (except in so far that Celtic and early Roman coins were a source of bullion to both sides), and we must think of the process as the exchange of British raw material for Mediterranean finished goods. What were these? The supply of Irish gold, so important in earlier times, had by now largely dried up; the tin trade, which many classical writers describe, had started as early as the sixth century B.C. and still continued with the tribes of south-west Britain. By the first century A.D. British exports, according to Strabo (iv, 5, 1-3) included 'corn, cattle, gold, silver, iron . . . hides, slaves and dogs useful for hunting'. In return, the La Tène princes of (unconquered) Britain in the first century B.C. were avid for prestige items of classical workmanship, and above all for wine, in amphorae. The state of the wine when it reached Britain can only be imagined, but it undoubtedly stimulated maritime and overland trade-routes that are currently being identified. Hengistbury Head in Dorset (Cunliffe, 1978) is convincingly recognised as the principal destination of the Roman ships, whose wrecks containing amphorae have been found at intervals off the coast of western France and in Guernsey, outside St. Peter Port. To this we could add a supposed Roman customs-house at Toulouse. Earlier in the first century some of this trade probably passed overland across the base of the Armorican peninsula, where inland amphora-finds might point to consumption en route as well as trade.

Between 100 and 50 B.C., then, close trading links were established between Britain and Armorica, with Guernsey lying on the most direct route. Archaeologically this is the 'first contact horizon', showing particularly in coinage (though the distribution of Armorican coins in Britain shows a one-way movement) and most of all in pottery: vessels with graphite coating over the exterior surface and vessels with finely-tooled cordons and grooves—both types evidently made in the Côtes-du-Nord and Ille-et-Vilaine region, and found both at Hengistbury and in the Guernsey cist-graves.

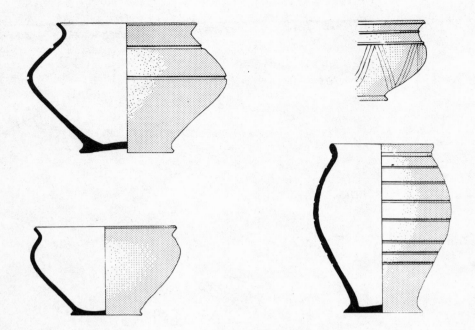

Fig. 23.   Wheelmade pottery from the Hougue au Comte, Guernsey, x ¼ (source:
Kendrick 1928).

Caesar's elimination of the Venetic navy in 56 B.C. may have freed the sea-routes
around Finistère, but it came too late. He had been campaigning in Gaul since 67 B.C.,
pursuing a policy of integrating the new province into the Roman world that continued
until 51 B.C. At this time the flow of imports to Hengistbury declined markedly,
showing the isolation of the south-western British markets and a re-direction of trade
to the south-eastern tribes, who may even have been given monopoly trading rights
by treaty. The effect in the Channel Islands was equally dramatic—a virtual isolation
from international contacts until the early years of the first century A.D. At this time
—the 'second cultural horizon'—a new range of imported pottery appeared, including
Spanish amphorae, Gallo-Roman samian, Romanised flagons, S. Remy ware and fine
black wares of Terra Nigra type. If an historical explanation is required, it is possible
that the reorganisation of Gaul under Augustus might have provided the occasion for
peaceful contacts to be resumed once more.

Two settlements excavated in Guernsey document this ebb and flow. The slightly
earlier site, in the King's Road, St. Peter Port, might have been a ditched, banjo-shaped
enclosure with two ditches, like antennae, forming a funnel-shaped entrance—a type
familiar in southern Britain. This excavation was barely complete when these words
were written, and the degree of overlap with the other site—Les Tranquesous—has
yet to be evaluated. The latter site, now fully published (Burns, 1977) apparently had
an earlier phase of occupation belonging to the period of isolation. This is distinct
from the second cultural phase which clearly marks a re-opening of trade with the
St. Malo region and perhaps beyond. The whole site, as traced from air-photographs
and selective excavation, will serve as a type-site for this period in the Islands (Fig. 24).
There is a straight double-ditched trackway, successive curvilinear enclosure-ditches
and several hut-circles with gullies, pits and hearths. In the fill of one ditch were

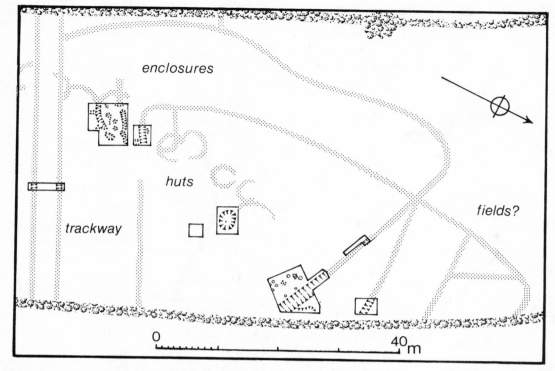

Fig. 24. Iron Age settlement at the Tranquesous, Guernsey; cropmarks and excavated features (source: Burns 1977).

found briquetage fragments that provide a useful link with the debris found on coastal salt-working sites throughout the Channel Islands. Characteristic exposures of this debris can be found, for example, in Western Guernsey at the Catioroc and the promontory of Fort le Crocq, and on the beach in Herm below Fisherman's Cottage. These are generally understood to be of Iron Age or Roman date, but rarely contain datable finds. The debris consists of soft, coarse brick fragments of the furnaces and boiling-pans for brine. Salt was evidently a commodity consumed—and apparently traded—in some quantity in the Gallo-Roman world. One such site has been excavated in Guernsey (Lihou, 1976). Another was examined in 1956, when analysis of the deposit on the bricks 'showed a high magnesium/sodium ratio, indicative of a calcined residue left after the evaporation of heated sea-water' (Frend, 1956).

At the northern end of the Tranquesous site are three small fields. We must assume that it is only the intensive cultivation of the Islands that has deprived us of evidence for 'Celtic fields' elsewhere. Possible traces of field-boundaries that might go back to the neolithic and Bronze Age have been noted. These might, of course, be Iron Age or even Roman; there is no doubt, however, about the Iron Age date of field-ditches that have appeared, cut into the burial-mound of Les Fouaillages that is currently under excavation.

Finally, to dispel the impression that Guernsey had a monopoly of Iron Age settlement, we should mention a hut-site excavated at St. Helier (*Annu. Bull. Soc. Jersiaise*, 22, 1977, 20-21). It was roughly rectangular, measuring about 3m. by 2m., with a clay floor, a hearth and stone pot-boilers, and it was set against a shingle bank. It was in an unusual position, on the edge of what is understood to have been the Iron Age shoreline. It must have been swept by the tide in bad weather, and was probably re-occupied seasonally. The clay floor had been renewed more than once, and the rear wall rebuilt. An interesting discovery was some carbonised remains of six-row barley—a known Celtic variety recorded for the first time in the Channel Islands. A sherd of pottery almost certainly imported from Brittany shows an incised scroll—a glimpse of the artistry that is sometimes to be found on later Iron Age pottery.

THE ROMAN PERIOD

Considering that the hand of Rome was felt in almost every part of north-west Europe, it is curious that the Channel Islands have so little to show for it. Nevertheless, there were many odd corners and areas at the fringe of the Empire where bureaucratic control was neither accepted nor enforced, but where Roman artifacts penetrated by the process known as 'drift'. Roman material is, in fact, found in some quantity in the Channel Islands; but it does not add up to true 'Romanisation'. We have seen that contact with the Roman world was renewed by the first century A.D. in the 'second contact horizon' The numerous late Republican coins (found in Gaulish hoards) do not invalidate the idea of a break during and after Caesar's day—though students of the unexpected will appreciate the suggestion (Stevens, 1979) that Jersey was a training-ground for Caesar's first expedition to Britain in 55 B.C.! What is clear from the evidence is that in the first century the Islands regained their role as staging-points in the sea-passages between Britain, Gaul and the Mediterranean world. Throughout the Roman period the point of departure in Gaul was Alet (St. Malo), while a road has been traced northwards from Chartres to the tip of the Cotentin peninsula, supposedly Claudian in date (Chevallier, 1976, 162). Boulogne, however, was adopted as the springboard for the invasion of Britain in A.D. 43.

Claudius' advisers may well have envisaged the use of this part of Gaul for an invigorated cross-Channel trade with Britain. In Augustus' day, we are told, the Britons were paying dues not only on imports from Gaul, but also on their own exports (Strabo, iv, 5, 1-3). Moreover, this particular route was already familiar to mariners. Clear evidence of this is the discovery of amphorae from at least one Roman wreck outside St. Peter Port, Guernsey, together with samian ware, mortarium and even remains of an anchor of Roman type (R. Keen, pers. comm.). It is thought that these ships were making for a harbour at St. Sampson. The amphorae are of Dressel type 2B, dating from the late first or early second century A.D. and coming from Spain; their contents were probably *garum* (fish-sauce) rather than wine. A further cargo was possibly salted fish, as it is known that in the second century this industry developed in Gaul, probably using barrels rather than amphorae (Sanquer and Galliou, 1972). Good supporting evidence has been found in excavations at the tiny harbour of Fishbourne, Sussex, in the form of discarded ship's ballast—schist of Breton type, sheared porphyrite and granodiorite, possibly from the Channel Islands, hornblende diorite from Jersey, and coarse arkosite sandstone from Alderney (Cunliffe, 1971, 2-3). A date late in the first century A.D. is possible for this, but not secure; it implies, however, that a ship discharged its cargo in the Channel Islands and took on ballast before setting off for Britain to load up with fresh cargo. Intermittent or regular contact of this kind will explain the frequent discoveries of Roman pottery in the Islands, both Gaulish (samian ware, for instance) or British (black-burnished ware from Dorset and grey wares from Alice Holt, Hampshire, have been identified in Jersey and Alderney). Indeed, at the Tranquesous site (where one amphora and an Aucissa brooch came to rest) an estimated 20 per cent. of the Roman pottery was imported. A flagon-neck, of second-century type, found at Maîtresse-Ile in the Ecrehous points to a direct route to Alet, where a major harbour and shipyard has been identified (Langouet, 1977).

Presumably the sailors had names for the Islands, but the identification of these is a matter of some dispute (Kendrick, 1928, 16). Jersey and Guernsey are popularly believed to have been named *Caesarea* and *Sarnia* respectively, but these are probably mistaken attributions from the Roman route-book, the *Antonine Itinerary*. In any case, Sarnia is a misreading of *Sarmia*, and Kendrick tentatively suggested another name in the *Itinerary, Andium*, for Jersey. Interestingly, the name 'Sarniensis' (i.e., 'native of Sarnia') is found on a bronze *diploma* found in Corsica in 1920, naming A. Basiel, son of Turbel, who served under Vespasian in the fleet based on Misenum, possibly served in the Jewish War and was demobilised as a veteran after it on 5 April, A.D. 71 (Bourde de la Rogerie, 1921). Interesting as it may be, however, this is hardly support for an identification of Sarnia with Guernsey.

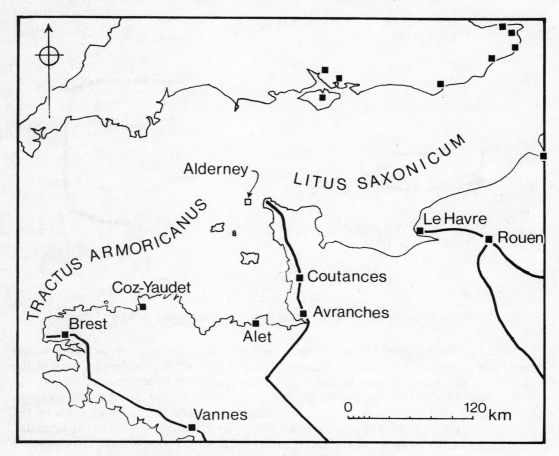

Fig. 25.   Coastal defence in the 3rd and 4th centuries A.D.

47

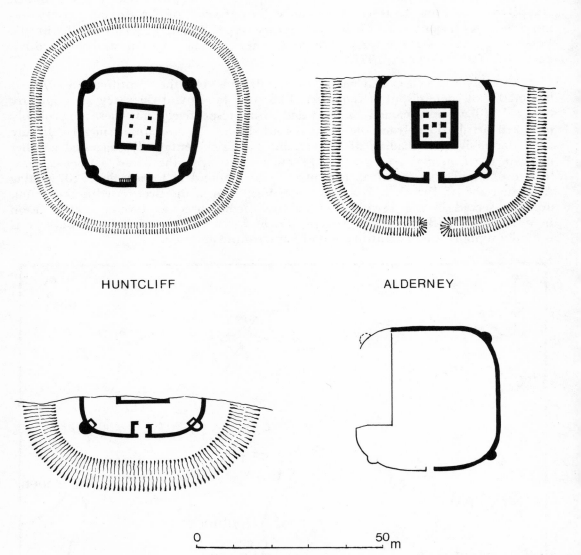

GOLDSBOROUGH   SCARBOROUGH

HUNTCLIFF   ALDERNEY

0   50 m

Fig. 26.   The Yorkshire signal-stations and the Nunnery, Alderney, compared (from Johnston 1977a).

Technically, the Channel Islands formed part of *Gallia Lugdunensis,* or *Lugdunensis Secunda* after A.D. 297 when this province formed part of the Diocese of Gaul in the Prefecture of the Gauls (which included Britain). The military reorganisation on both sides of the Channel is recorded in a late document, the *Notitia Dignitatum,* which gives us in some detail the military dispositions for this part of Gaul in the later years of the Empire. These were years when piracy, long endemic in the Channel, got out of control—in spite of the impressive fortifications on both coasts which are so massive that some scholars have suggested that more than piracy was at stake. Two series of coastal forts and signalling towers in Britain and Gaul comprise the *Litus Saxonicum,* or Saxon Shore, with a further system along the coast of Armorica,

1. (left) La Cotte de St. Brelade, Jersey. The arch giving entrance to the cave (to the left), in 1954. Note the depth of unexcavated deposits. (Photo: R. F. Le Sueur)

2. (below) Post-glacial deposits near Tourgis, Alderney. The granitic rock surface has been fractured by frost and water percolation. (Photo: author)

The 'submerged forest' of St. Ouen's Bay, at very low tide. (Photo: author)

4. La Pouquelaye de Faldouet, Jersey. An engraving of *c.* 1840, after the removal of the mound, but before the 'restoration' of 1868.

5. The site as it is today. (Photo: author)

La Sergenté, Jersey.

The ruined structure on the beach at Oyster Point, Herm. (Photo: author)

8.   Le Mont de la Ville, Jersey. An engraving of 1787, before the removal of the monument.

9.   The same monument re-erected at Park Place, Henley. An engraving of 1802.

Four Lukis drawings from the *Collectanea*

10. (*top left*) Le Creux ès Faïes, Guernsey.

11. (*top right*) Les Pourciaux North, Alderney, 1853, showing the miniature cists with their contents.

12. (*bottom left*) La Roche Que Sonne, Guernsey, 1837.

13. (*bottom right*) Iron Age cists on the Catioroc, Guernsey, 1848.

14.   La Varde, Guernsey, an engraving of *c.* 1840, before the mound was restored.

15.   Le Trépied, Guernsey. (Photo: author)

16. Ville-ès-Nouaux, Jersey. In the foreground is the cist with stone circle. In the distance, the gallery-grave. (Photo: author)

17. Les Monts Grantez, Jersey. Capstones of the passage and chamber, with the side-chamber to the right. (Photo: author)

18. Le Perron du Roi, Guernsey. (Photo: author)

19. La Gran' Mère du Chimquière, Guernsey.
(Photo: E. Sirett)

20. Possible statue-menhir, discovered in Sark in 1980. Scale in half-metre intervals. (Photo: author)

21. La Longue Rocque, Guernsey. (Photo: author)

22. La Dame Blanche, Jersey. (Photo: author)

23.   The Tourgis Dolmen, Alderney, before excavation. (Photo: author)

24.   The same site, as excavated. The capstone has been temporarily removed (far left). 2-metre scale. (Photo: author)

25. La Vermandaye, Little Sark. (Photo: author)

26. Clouet Bay, Little Sark. The partly-collapsed cist. 2-metre scale. (Photo: author)

27.   The Pinnacle, Jersey. (Photo: author)

28.   View from the Pinnacle Rock, after the excavation of the site. (Photo: E. F. Guiton)

29.   The Ile Agois, looking north. The habitation sites were on the crest and the far end of the island. (Photo: author)

30.   The earthwork at Câtel, Jersey. (Photo: author)

31.   Longis Common, Alderney, from Essex Hill. The Nunnery is in the middle distance, with the area of Roman settlement to the left of it. Iron Age settlement has been excavated at The Kennels (the white house to the left) and Les Huguettes (extreme far left of picture). The two sites of Les Pourciaux are in the distance, left. (Photo: author)

32.   The Nunnery. Fallen bastion (period I) on the beach. Scale in feet. (Photo: author)

33. The gold torque from St. Helier, Jersey. (Photo: Société Jersiaise)

34. Pottery from Les Huguettes, Alderney. (Photo: Alderney Society)

. *Phalera* from the Sark Hoard, a drawing intended r engraving. (Photo: Society of Antiquaries)

36. A bone gaming-piece from the Cobo long-house, Guernsey, showing a stylised dragon. Guernsey Museum. (Photo: author)

7. (*above*) A sherd of imported French pot- ry from the Cobo long-house. Guernsey useum. (Photo: author)

3. (*right*) The Observatory of the Lukis ouse in St. Peter Port, now the headquarters f the Archaeological Group of the Société uernesiaise. (Photo: author)

39.   Monku, Herm. The massive blocks of structure no. 11, disturbed by quarrying. (Photo: author)

40.   Granite-quarrying in Herm at the foot of Le Petit Monceau about 1870. The lost structure no. 5 once stood roughly where this picture was taken.

the *Tractus Armoricanus*. The Channel Islands come at the eastern end of the latter. Fig. 25 shows the sites recorded in the *Notitia* and identified from archaeological remains or clues (Johnson, 1976, ch. 5); a further unnamed site at Coz Yaudet is known from substantial masonry remains (Sanquer, 1977, 50, and Plate XVI). This leaves a gap between Coutances and Rouen (which is strictly in the Saxon Shore), since no fort has been found on the Cotentin; and it brings us to the disputed Roman origins of the Nunnery fort in Alderney (pp. 133-5) which on the map has a strong claim for consideration as the anchor-point of the Tractus Amoricanus. The difficulties have recently been discussed (Johnston, 1971 and 1977a) and need only be summarised here; the use or re-use of Roman material in the fabric and the herring-bone masonry are not indicators of Roman date, though the use of largely undressed stone sets the Nunnery apart from the forts of Norman or later date where ashlar is used. The substantial offset just below ground level is a Roman technique. Comparison of the plan with the five signal-stations of the Yorkshire coast (Fig. 26) supports a Roman date for the single entrance, gently rounded corners and functionally insignificant bastions. Nearby was found the bronze buckle (Fig. 27) provisionally identified by Mrs. S. Hawkes (in pers. comm.) as a military type of the third century. This is a prototype of the classic zoomorphic forms that are often associated with the Saxon Short forts; in other words, the buckle might indicate an official Roman presence in Alderney. On the other hand, the lack of evidence for a ditch or central tower invites caution—points that we hope to settle by excavation before long. The size, moreover, is anomalous; it is larger than the normal signal-towers and smaller than the Welsh fort of Caer Gybi, with which it has been compared (Kendrick, 1928, 257). Perhaps it had a double role, of signal-station and naval base. Longis Bay (before the causeway to Raz Island was built) would have formed an ideal natural harbour for the fleet in its operations against the pirates. The biggest problem, however, is its position so close to sea-level; Essex Hill, which overlooks Longis Bay, would be a better site, above the lowest fog-banks and visible from the other Islands and Cap de la Hague, the nearest point on the French mainland. This last, too, would be an ideal site as it lies at the head of the road leading inland along the Cotentin peninsula towards major bases at Coutances and Avranches; in much the same way the Yorkshire signal-stations were placed for inland, as well as lateral communication—an early-warning system, in fact. The double row of wooden piles, running from the beach and under the foundations of the Nunnery, could be interpreted as a landing-stage (Kendrick, 1928, 256).

Roman occupation debris (now lost and undatable) has been noted under the Nunnery itself (Durtnell, 1966) and there is no doubt that on Longis Common there was· a substantial settlement of early date. The earliest coin is of Gaius Caligula (A.D. 37–41), followed by those of Trajan (A.D. 98–117), and Hadrian (A.D. 117–138). Pottery, recorded and illustrated by Kendrick, but now untraceable, was of the first century; this accompanied a cremation in a chest with iron fittings found in 1928. More recently, the rescue excavation at the Kennels on Longis Common (unpublished) produced a quantity of late first- and early second-century samian. The black-burnished ware noted above is also of early date (D. Williams in pers. comm.), and cremations in urns have been recorded, near the Nunnery and elsewhere on the Common. This may not be the only area of Roman settlement in Alderney, as a find of six sherds of widely-ranging dates examined recently suggests another site in St. Anne's at the other end of the Island. Kendrick sets out the tenuous evidence for substantial Roman buildings on Longis Common. Two

Fig. 27. Late Roman
bronze buckle.

Fig. 28. Diagram of a typical Romano-Celtic
square temple. The structure at the Pinnacle,
Jersey, was probably of this general type.

long walls ran east-west and north-south, associated with buildings that had
identifiable rooms. The debris included roof-tiles of Roman pattern with what
sounded like stone sockets for doors. The position of these discoveries is lost,
and they have probably been destroyed by coastal erosion and the war-time
construction of a huge sea-wall. The later phases are represented by the contents
of a rubbish-pit near the Nunnery, excavated in 1889 and recently re-examined
(Johnston, 1977a). These included fragments of nearly a hundred pots, a glass bead,
some pieces of glass, bricks and tiles, iron nails, two bronze finger-rings, a bronze
thimble, a piece of bone comb, three bronze pins, a coin of Commodus, and the
bronze buckle in Fig. 27. How, then, do we explain this substantial but undefended
settlement in such a vulnerable position? If the Nunnery is indeed Roman, then the
settlement will have been protected in its later years; if, on the other hand, there
was no Imperial presence in the Island, then a very different explanation becomes
possible: in view of the remoteness and inaccessibility of Alderney, could we be
looking at the material remains not of the Roman fleet, but of the very pirates that
the fleet existed to deal with?

Remoteness may also help to explain one further structure, unquestionably of
Roman date—the rectangular building of The Pinnacle, Jersey (p. 86 and Plate 27).
The two concentric walls were dated to the Roman period by pottery (which
included some black-burnished ware) and a coin of Commodus (A.D. 180–191).
Some flimsy structures outside the building (now vanished) were thought to be
outbuildings. It was thought at first to be a guard-house for a signal-post on The
Pinnacle rock, and it would indeed be possible, in fine weather, to signal to Alderney.
Frequent fog, would, of course, lessen its usefulness, but the same conditions would
preclude the movement of ships which it is assumed would be the function of the
signal-post to report. The excavators (Godfray and Burdo, 1950) concluded, probably
correctly, that this was a Romano-Celtic temple. The central rectangle would be the
cella, or shrine, the outer foundations supporting an outer wall or verandah at a

lower level (Fig. 28). Such temples in the Roman world were circular, polygonal or square, rarely oblong; and the only substantial find was an iron object resembling a plough-coulter. This complete absence of the normal dedicatory objects is a very strong argument against its identification as a temple. The whole area was meticulously excavated and nothing will have been missed—a point, incidentally, that has escaped the treasure-hunters who have recently uprooted even the foundations in their fruitless search for loot. Nevertheless, its very remoteness would be typical of many rural shrines in out-of-the-way places. No associated settlement is known, though the site is accessible by sea. St. Ouen's Bay, unsuitable as a harbour, is ideal for beaching boats. The choice of site may have been influenced by the nearby spring; for such Romano-Celtic shrines often perpetuated the Celtic veneration of spirits resident in rocks and water.

We might end with two Roman objects in Jersey which are, without any doubt, imports to the Island in recent times. The first is the 'Roman Pillar' in St. Lawrence's church (p. 53) which was plundered in antiquity from a villa or public building and re-used in c. A.D. 600 as a gravestone (Stevens, 1975). The other is a small portable altar of stone with the inscription VETERIBVS SV . . . ('to the ancient gods') (R.I.B., 1669). It was actually found at Chesterholme, on Hadrian's Wall, and brought to Jersey by a descendant of the family that found it. Its whereabouts is unknown, and it eluded an intensive search in Jersey in 1971. But it should be borne in mind as it will cause considerable interest when it eventually comes to light again.

THE MIGRATION PERIOD

We have seen that, in the later years of the Roman Empire, the Channel was a route for the seaborne movements of many peoples, official and unofficial, raiders and settlers. Nevertheless, one major element in the settlement of south Britain, the Anglo-Saxons, is missing from Brittany and the Channel Islands; moreover, the far-reaching operations of Viking raiders and settlers in the ninth century and later seem to have left little evidence for North Sea contacts, beyond the unproven suggestion that La Hougue Bie (like other tombs, perhaps) was plundered by them, and the story that St. Magloire's monastic community in Sark was abruptly, if only temporarily, ended by a Viking raid. The common place-name *Hougue*, here as in Normandy used for a mound or barrow, is derived from the Old Norse *Haugr* (eminence), and is the same as *How* in northern England and Scotland. The *Bie* of Hougue Bie (and Hambye in Normandy) is related to the *-by* ending of English and Scandinavian place-names for a homestead or settlement. These place-names may be the most enduring legacy from a people who are noted for the scarcity of their archaeological traces overseas.

In the half-century after A.D. 500, Gallo-Roman 'Armorica' became Celtic 'Brittany'—a clear indication of the permanence of the extensive immigration from south-west Britain. It has been urged by N. Chadwick (1969, 190–1) that not only Anglo-Saxon pressures in most of Britain, but more particularly the menace of a pincer-movement from Ireland encouraged the inhabitants of central, south and west Wales and the Devon-Cornwall peninsula to take to their curraghs and follow their leaders to Brittany. This migration—epitomised by the 12,000 colonists allegedly brought by Riothamus in *c.* 470—brought with it a Celtic language (marked, for instance, by the Breton parish-names in *plou*) and a distinctive form of of Celtic Christianity. The process of settlement was at its height in the first half of the sixth century, but continued through the seventh into the eighth. The transformation was largely peaceful, and the five pre- and Gallo-Roman *civitates* of Armorica were metamorphosed, over several centuries, into the nine Roman *dioceses* adopted after the Council of Tours. For the sixth century was the 'Age of Saints'—the *sancti* of Welsh origin on the whole, who were largely monks leading their followers to found small eremitic communities often in inaccessible places like Sark, and perhaps the Ile Agois, Jersey. St. Tudual, for instance, whose name is preserved in the dedication of the (later) chapel on Herm, is known to have originated in Cornish Dumnonia; most importantly, St. Samson, who was a student at Llantwit Major and a native of Dyfed, gathered his followers in Gwent and Cornwall en route to found the Breton community and abbey of Dol, where he became its first abbot. Abbots, in the Celtic church, were more important than bishops; the latter were more peripatetic, based on monasteries rather than the cathedrals that had dioceses on the

Roman pattern. Parishes took shape around the new communities and were, it seems, a secular rather than an ecclesiastical creation. The Channel Islands shared the general spread of Celtic Christian settlements in the region, though the saints' names, such as St. Helier, cannot yet be tied down to physical archaeological remains; even St. Magloire, whose move from Dol to a new community in Sark is dated precisely to A.D. 565, has so far eluded the archaeologists, though the site of the water-mill can still be identified (Ewen and de Carteret, 1969, 16–17). The extant structures by the Seigneurie (p. 126) are those of a medieval monastery. All the Channel Islands were in the diocese of the Bishop of Coutances, who retained his ecclesiastical jurisdiction over them until A.D. 1567.

The story of the Channel Islands in the migration period was substantially that of Brittany, characterised by P. R. Giot (1960, 205) as 'protohistory with practically no archaeological evidence'. We might add that solid documentary evidence before the 11th century in Brittany is also lacking. The picture is that of a jigsaw known in outline, of which we have only half-a-dozen coloured pieces that do not interlock and could fit almost anywhere. Scholars have made the most of the linguistic and documentary sources; the only deliberate attempt to look for a missing piece has been the excavation on the Ile Agois, Jersey (Finlaison and Holdsworth, 1979). Between 20 and 25 stone-built hut-circles and a landward parapet wall have been identified on this islet (Plate 29, Fig. 43) accessible today only at low tide and with a fresh-water spring at the base of the rock. It may have been severed from the mainland of Jersey as late as the post-medieval period. Casual exploitation from neolithic to Roman times was suggested by the finds which indicated a date into the ninth century for the structures. The interpretation of this remote and undefended settlement as an eremitic community is strengthened by comparison with similar 'monastic' sites in the Northern Isles and Ireland, where the community frequently had a stone oratory or chapel, corresponding to one of the two rectangular buildings dominating the Ile Agois. In particular, several promontory sites in Brittany, also thought to be Iron Age, have been re-dated by excavation to this period. If the interpretation is correct, the Ile Agois gives some archaeological substance to the known but elusive settlements by 'saints' in Sark and elsewhere in the Islands.

The conversion of the Channel Islands has left no other architectural traces, for the supposedly 'early' chapels, such as the Fishermen's Chapel at St. Brelade, Jersey, and that of St. Apolline, Guernsey, cannot be earlier (in their present form at least) than the beginning of the 12th century (Lemprière, 1980). In A.D. 422 the Council of Arles had passed Canon 23, which aimed 'to extirpate the custom of worshipping springs, trees, stones' and prompted, at some unknown date, the 'christianising' of prehistoric menhirs with a carved cross (pp. 101, 105). Built into a house in the Rue des Messuriers, St. Peter Port, is a stone carved with a cross whose arms end in circles containing crosslets, datable perhaps to the eighth century (McCormack, 1977). This may once have been the upright grave-marker of a missionary 'saint' or priest; so, too, may be the 'Roman Pillar' in St. Lawrence's church, Jersey, tentatively identified by C. G. Stevens (1975) as a grave-stone of *c.* A.D. 600. The pillar may well be Roman, but the whole thing could be a medieval or post-medieval import to the Island.

Two loose pieces of the jigsaw remain. One is two sherds of a *bar-lip* pot found at Longis, Alderney, in white sand at a depth of 8ft. (Durtnell, 1930, 2 (Fig. 29)). These cooking-pots have a distinctive ear-like spout and a bar for suspension, and are found in Holland and Cornwall (Dunning, 1959, 48-9). Petrological examination has shown

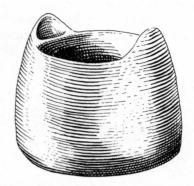

Fig. 29.   Bar-lip pottery; left a sherd from Alderney, x ½; right, a typical
cooking pot.

this specimen to be either local, or more probably Cornish. The type is of ninth-tenth-century date. The second is a *long-house* partly excavated at Cobo, Guernsey, in 1967 and unpublished. The general type is shown diagrammatically in Fig. 30.

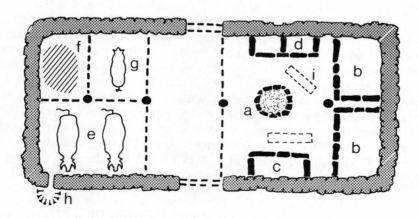

Fig. 30.   Diagram of a typical long-house; examples in Guernsey and Jersey were probably of this general type. a) hearth; b) box-beds; c, d) children/storage; e) cattle; f) fodder; g) pig/calf; h) drain; i) benches.

Some Breton examples are discussed by G. I. Merion-Jones (1973 a, b), and a comparable Cornish example at Mawgan Porth is described by R. L. S. Bruce-Mitford (1956). Double (opposed) entrances are frequently found, and internal arrangements vary considerably. In later examples the open hearth is replaced by a fireplace and chimney at the gable end. Inhabited Breton examples have been recorded in the 20th century, and the earliest recorded is of the 12th century. At Cobo, the most important single find was a bone gaming-piece (Plate 36) depicting a highly stylised dragon; this and the pottery (Plate 37), one sherd of which resembles 'Normandy Gritty Ware', would place this dwelling somewhere in the 11th or 12th centuries A.D.

Part of a rather later but similar building of long-house form (dated to the first half of the 13th century) has been excavated in St. Helier (Finlaison, 1976). With these two sites of the historic period we must leave the prehistory and protohistory of the Channel Islands as we stand on the threshold of the full medieval period.

ANTIQUITIES AND SCHOLARS

The most enduring prehistoric antiquities in the Islands are undoubtedly the megaliths, and it was to these (and their contents) that the early antiquaries directed their attentions. Indeed, it was thanks principally to the energies of the Guernsey family of Lukis—father, three daughters, and four sons—that much of the earliest speculation in Europe about megaliths centred on the Channel Islands examples. The father, Frederick Corbin Lukis (1788-1871) was the true pioneer, self-taught and dedicated to the collection of information on anything from meteorology to anthropology. His interests were international, and so were his connections. His correspondence with the celebrated Danish archaeologist, Worsaae, preserved in Copenhagen, contains meticulous copies of his drawings and plans of Channel Islands finds; the family collections, bequeathed to Guernsey in 1907 and now the nucleus of the present museum, illustrate his world-wide view of prehistory and megalithic monuments. He was among the first to realise that the stone 'dolmens' and 'cromlechs' were not Druidic sacrificial altars but tombs, and that the pots and other objects were deposited as part of a funerary ritual (1848, 326–8). He published little, but left a treasure-house of notes and assorted papers and six great leather-bound volumes of manuscript, the *Collectanea Antiqua* (largely illustrated by his daughter, Mary Anne) that are now preserved in Guernsey. His eldest son, Frederick Collings Lukis, carried the analysis further, seeing the megaliths as evidence for a comprehensive pattern of migration and diffusion to include Asia, Africa and North America 'quitting the high lands of Central Asia, at a very early period, soon subdivided and subdivided, passing in radiating lines to various countries, and conveying the same customs, whether for ceremonial, sepulchral or domestic purposes' (1853, 235). This view was quite tenable until the 'radiocarbon revolution' of recent years, and is still true on a modified and more regional scale (p. 86). The Lukis family were, in fact, early 'rescue archaeologists', hurrying to any site that was reported to be in danger, even purchasing sites to save them from the quarrymen's hammer. The interest that their discoveries aroused moved the Ethnological Society of London to commission a report on the state of the prehistoric monuments in the Islands from Lieutenant S. P. Oliver, R.A. The 'Oliver Report' (1870), in which J. W. Lukis had a hand, thus became the first illustrated survey of Channel Island megaliths to be published. A full bibliography of the Lukis family's publications is given by Kendrick (1928, 100–102), and an appreciation of the family by a descendant, E. F. Lukis (1974).

Three years after the Oliver Report (in 1873) the Société Jersiaise was founded and the new museum in Pier Road opened its doors; subsequently enlarged with the addition of the Barreau Art Gallery it has recently moved its archaeological collections and workrooms to a new museum at La Hougue Bie, but it remains one of the ·few major museums owned and staffed by a Society. Early numbers of its *Bulletin Annuel* show that antiquaries, notably E. C. Cable, were excavating enthusiastically, if unskilfully, on the dolmens. Incidentally, Cable's report on the Beauport Dolmen (1877) must contain one of the earliest chemical soil analyses on record, indicating a cremation. The year 1893 saw the first *Transactions* of the Société Guernesiaise (originally the Guernsey Society of Natural Science) and in 1907 Francis du Bois Lukis, who had inherited his father's collections, bequeathed them to the States of Guernsey. They immediately purchased the family house in St. Peter Port to display them as a museum. The collections were subsequently moved to the redundant chapel of St. Barnabas not far away, and are now in the fine new museum in Candie Gardens; today the house is Government offices, but it is pleasant to note that the Archaeological Group of the Société now occupies the picturesque Observatory in the grounds (Plate 38) as its headquarters. The Société Guernesiaise, like its Jersey counterpart, is large and influential, and both of them own and conscientiously maintain several of the principal prehistoric monuments of their respective islands. But for Guernsey the bequest of the Lukis collections was the crucial beginning of a close liaison in archaeological research between the States and the Société that continues in some notable excavations today, and culminated in 1977 with the creation of the Museum and Art Gallery in Candie Gardens—a miniature masterpiece of modern architecture with a full-time staff and an imaginative display that earned it the coveted Museum of the Year Award. A similar liaison of Société and States in Jersey has long been the subject of delicate negotiations that have borne fruit archaeologically only in quite recent years.

The decades before and after the First World War were a Golden Age for archaeology in both Islands. In Guernsey the names of the Rev. G. E. Lee and Major S. Carey Curtis are associated with excavations small and great (L'Islet, for instance in 1912) and the discovery of the important carvings at le Déhus in 1919. In Jersey, J. Sinel, R. R. Marrett, and E. T. Nicolle began the excavations at La Cotte de St. Brelade, and in 1924 La Hougue Bie was purchased and its spectacular chambered tomb revealed. At The Pinnacle, from 1930–1935, Fr. C. Burdo and Major A. D. B. Godfray excavated what remains today the most important prehistoric settlement in the Islands. Dolmens, menhirs and coin-hoards were excavated and published with increasing professionalism, the reports being illustrated with beautiful drawings from the pen of Major N. L. V. Rybot. By 1928 the scene was set for the first volume of *The Archaeology of the Channel Islands,* a meticulous survey by T. D. Kendrick that remains a classic of its kind. Kendrick, in fact, published only Volume I (*The Bailiwick of Guernsey*), passing the Jersey material he had collected to Jacquetta Hawkes, who completed Volume II (*The Bailiwick of Jersey*) by 1937. This time, publication was to be by the Société Jersiaise; but funds proved insufficient, and the book appeared (with an undated title page) only in 1939. Each volume, in its day, represented the most up-to-date modern scholarship and together they form a landmark in European archaeology.

A sign, however, that the Golden Age was passing was the privately sponsored 're-excavation' and reconstruction of the Déhus in 1932-3 by archaic methods at the hands of a specialist in the occult convinced that it was Iron Age in date (Collum 1933). Nevertheless, this lapse of judgment was soon eclipsed by Jacquetta Hawkes' publication, and the only significant excavation in the Islands (La Cotte) continued until it was interrupted by the outbreak of war and the German occupation. In the post-war recovery and prosperity of the Islands archaeological research remained dormant, as can be seen from the contents of both *Bulletin* and *Transactions*; these were lean years archaeologically, relieved by one serious excavation—the first of a planned four seasons on the earthwork at Frémont Point, Jersey, in 1964—and the formation of an Archaeological Section of the Société Jersiaise. Four years later, however, the *Bulletin* reported that 'the Section again finds itself in the position of having no-one resident in the Island who can direct an excavation'—a situation that was tacitly admitted in Guernsey, too. With the help of Southampton University, a training school in excavation and field survey was held in Jersey in 1970, and a fresh survey of the megaliths proposed by both Sociétés (Johnston forthcoming); lecturers, specialists and excavation directors were sent out from England for a new phase of research excavations, while a growing alarm at the losses caused by urban development in St. Helier culminated in an outspoken survey (Finlaison, 1975) and a series of rescue excavations under particularly trying circumstances. Revival in Guernsey came more slowly, but with growing confidence and expertise the new Archaeological Group has embarked on field-walking, building-recording and some major excavations, notably at The Château des Marais, Les Tranquesous, Jerbourg and Les Fouaillages. Post-excavation work and conservation are now undertaken in the Islands themselves, a major advance in this respect being the formation of the Federation of Channel Islands Museums. The revival was felt also in Alderney, where the monuments had suffered seriously during the war-time evacuation of the civilian population and the conversion of the entire island into a fortified prison by the Germans. Here the Alderney Society is committed to a programme of re-discovery and study of the Island's antiquities and publishes a regular *Bulletin*. A small display of material in the Island Hall in 1968 soon grew into a full museum in new premises, encouraged by the Society's excavation of the Iron Age site at Les Huguettes which was followed by three further excavations, notably that of the Tourgis Dolmen—the first excavation, incidentally, to be commemorated on a postage stamp. In Sark, 1974 saw the formation of the Societé Sercquiaise and the re-discovery of two lost dolmens, leading to the first excavation in the Island, in 1980.

The longest and most important excavation ever undertaken in the Islands is that by the Société Jersiaise at La Cotte de St. Brelade. Begun in 1914, the work was assisted by grants from the British Association until 1918, when it was thought that the lowest levels had been reached. Following a theory, however, that there was more to find, Fr. Christian Burdo directed a second series of excavations that lasted, with a war-time gap from 1940–1950, until 1958. By then he had recognised, and later published (1959) the earlier occupation levels; the unfinished work was next taken up by the late Professor Charles McBurney and the Cambridge University Department of Archaeology and Anthropology in 1960, and the fossil beach was reached in 1961. By 1978 the programme was completed, and most of the 50m. of deposits in the cave had been removed. Protective works have now been taken to preserve the remaining sample from erosion. The post-excavation work, which is a joint undertaking of the Société Jersiaise, Cambridge University and the British Academy, will take some years yet; this collaboration is a measure of the international importance of the work. The finds and records will finally return to Jersey and—if the appeal is successful—will be housed in a new Arthur Mourant Institute for Archaeology and Geology, where subsequent research on them can be pursued. Throughout this complicated operation the Société has maintained its support.

Archaeology in the Channel Islands has indeed come of age. A mere 12 years has passed since the call for help was heard in 1968, and the record of growth must be unparalleled in any European country. There are few professional archaeologists in the Islands; the work is very British in its spirit of amateur work to professional standards, and utterly typical of the Channel Islands in its independence. To say this is not to underrate the generosity with which specialists in Britain and France have helped, and the considerable support from the States of Guernsey, Jersey and Alderney. The Press in both main Islands has played its part—not least in recording the prehistoric antics of Stone De Croze, The Original Guernseyman, wearing only a guernsey and a stone battle-axe, who appears each week in the *Guernsey Evening Press and Star*. Frederick Corbin Lukis would surely have smiled.

PART 2

SITES AND MONUMENTS

SITES AND MONUMENTS

JERSEY

JERSEY IS THE LARGEST of the Channel Islands, with an area of about 114 sq. km., compared with Guernsey's 64 sq. km. Although it is slightly nearer to Normandy than to Brittany, the cultural influences of the latter (in the Neolithic, at least) were the stronger. Roughly rectangular in outline, the island has a coast of often spectacular contrasts, from the precipitous and scenic cliffs of the north to the large, sheltered bay of St. Aubin in the south, and its smaller neighbour, St. Brelade. Most of the west coast comprises the generous sandy sweep of St. Ouen's Bay that ends abruptly in the storm-swept northern tip where The Pinnacle is gradually becoming an offshore rock and the cliffs of Grosnez bear a ruined castle and a lighthouse. The whole island tilts gently southwards from the granites, conglomerate and volcanic rocks of the rugged northern and north-eastern coasts to the lower south-west and south-east angles; the centre of the island has been carved into deep wooded valleys by five rivers that flow south into St. Aubin's Bay. The reason why Jersey is the only island to show occupation in the Palaeolithic period have been explained above (pp. 8-9). The loess-like deposits and 'head' overlying the varied hard rocks that are seldom far below the surface made most of the rest available in subsequent periods for cultivation and settlement, and provided a stable material for earthworks such as neolithic burial mounds and promontory forts of the Iron Age. The absence of substantial Roman settlement is hard to explain, except as the result of navigational hazards. Nevertheless, Jersey was undoubtedly a convenient stopping-point for Gallo-Roman merchants and later for Celtic 'saints' on the sea-routes between north-west France and Britain.

On the whole, structural monuments have survived the ages in reasonable condition, and our known losses are relatively few. Intensive cultivation, however, has deprived us of the settlements that are essential for understanding the monuments. Scatters of flint and pottery are sometimes exposed by ploughing and the shifting erosion of the dunes of St. Ouen; moreover, megalithic tombs and bronze hoards must bear some relationship to the settlement pattern. Three lost dolmens are not listed here—La Hougue Mauger and La Hougue de Forêt (both sacrificed to modern houses at 6019 5518 and 5730 4800 respectively) and Le Mont de la Ville which made way for Fort Regent in St. Helier. Other lost and doubtful sites are noted by Hawkes (1939) and Mourant (1966), including several possible menhirs. For the Hougue Mauger see Baal and Sinel (1915).

Access to sites is easy, provided courtesy and consideration are used. Some are owned by the States, others by the Société Jersiaise, and these are well maintained. The Société's museum is in St. Helier, but their Archaeological Museum was recently opened, with stores, workrooms and laboratory, in the grounds of La Hougue Bie.

The arrangement of sites is by parishes, and within this the order is based on proximity, in the belief that the reader will be visiting more than one site at a time. Those with private or hired cars will find the roads of the Island intricate and heavily used. Bus routes are numerous, radiating from the Weighbridge in St. Helier and following the valleys northwards. It is therefore impossible by bus to circumnavigate the island, to follow the north coast, or to cross the island from west to east. There is now no railway.

References are to the current official map at 1:2,500, published by the States of Jersey. A new one is in preparation (on which the sites will be correctly placed).

PARISH OF GROUVILLE

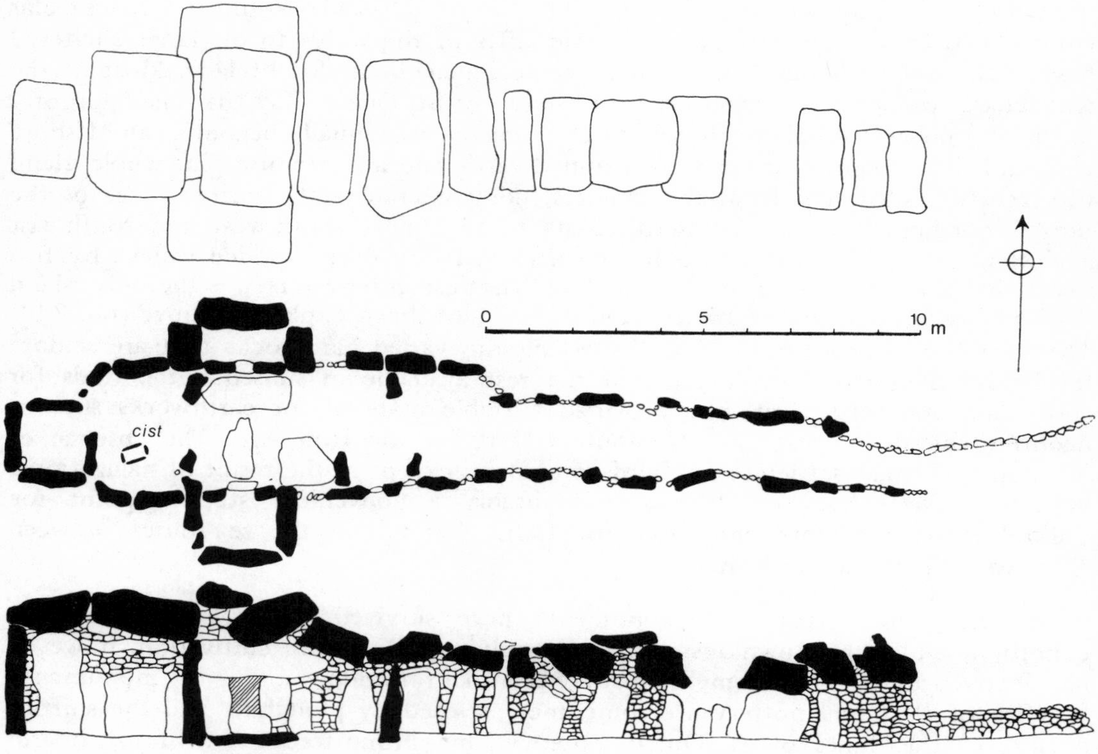

Fig. 31. La Hougue Bie (source: Baal et al 1925). Note slightly reduced scale.

La Hougue Bie
6285038

No. 3a bus to La Hougue Bie. The entrance to the site and museum is to the west of the T-junction.

La Hougue Bie is easily the most spectacular prehistoric monument in the Channel Islands, and in its sheer size and perfect preservation ranks alongside the great tombs of Brittany, the Orkneys, and the Boyne Valley of Ireland.

The circular mound, 54.9m. in diameter and 12.2m. high bears the weight of a conjoined pair of medieval chapels which in turn were crowned, until 1924, by an extraordinary pseudo-Gothic house, La Tour d'Auvergne. This colossal man-made mound contains, as far as is known, a single cruciform passage-grave, the main chamber of which lies immediately below its summit. The chambers are approached by a long passage 9.7m. long, the total length being 20.4m.; this is connected by a short funnel-like entrance to the original circumference of the mound. The dry-stone walling of this, and of that between the uprights of the interior, is original. The passage varies in breadth from 0.9–1.5m., and is generally about 1.4m. high, though at two points it rises to 2m. and one can stand upright. The passage, like the chambers, is roofed with flat capstones chosen for their size and rectangular shape.

The passage opens into the main chamber, some 2.5–3.6m. wide, 2m. high, and over 9m. long. The five capstones are partly supported by five uprights and a modern granite column. Two virtually identical side-chambers and a large end-chamber complete the cruciform plan, with an additional small cell at the very end. Each side-chamber is roofed by a single capstone, on which rest two capstones of the main chamber. The entrances to the side-chambers are framed by uprights forming narrow doorways, each with a raised sill level with the chamber floors. These doorways were probably closed by the two large slabs found lying on the floor of the main chamber, a third flat stone is unexplained, unless it too closed the cell at the end. This final cell, named 'the sanctuary' by the excavators (who, incidentally, provided it with a sill that they supposed was missing), is remarkable in its design and workmanship. It is square, its entrance is off-centre, the large stones appear to be specially selected and the dry-stone walling is of the finest workmanship. Its special significance eludes us; although it is unique in the Channel Islands, it can be paralleled at New Grange, in Ireland, and at Maes Howe in the Orkneys. The pre-eminence of the whole among the tombs of Jersey has been discussed above (p. 31). The only decoration that can be seen is series of cup-markings on the east upright of the north side-chamber and the underside of its capstone. Most of these, it should be noted, were hidden behind the dry-stone walling.

The mound, of earth, limpet shells, and rubble, must have lost 3m. or so of its summit when the chapels were built, and the foot of it has spread somewhat. This has never been investigated, but is believed to conceal a peristalith, or kerb of uprights—even with one or two now vanished free-standing outliers.

The excavators in 1924 were disappointed to discover that the tomb had already been ransacked at an unknown date, possibly by Viking treasure-seekers. Nevertheless, the original dry-stone blocking of the passage was intact (a rare feature to survive). A recent reappraisal suggests that the robbers broke in through the upper northern part of it. The scanty finds comprised fragmentary vase-supports, sherds of a probable plain beaker, worked flints, two beads and scattered human bones. Considering the size of the tomb, it is likely that it had not been used to capacity.

The name of the monument preserves the name of a Lady of Hambye in Normandy who, according to legend, built the mound and the first chapel over the grave of her husband; he had successfully slain a dragon lurking in the marshes of St. Lawrence, only to be himself murdered by a treacherous servant. The first chapel no doubt christianised a pagan mound, the second being added in 1520 to become the scene of some dubious miracles. Both suffered in the Dissolution, but provided sound foundations for d'Auvergne's picturesque folly. This structure came to be seen as an affront by the archaeologists of the Société, who demolished it with silent relish in 1924. The dolmen became their prize possession, and the new museum is now the focus of the island's archaeological work.

Publication: the full excavation report is by Baal and others (1925); additional material will be found in Mourant (1933 and 1974).

PARISH OF ST. BRELADE

La Cotte de St. Brelade   5929470

Owing to its dangerous nature, this site is now locked and closed to the public. There is no access from the beach. The site and the results of excavations are discussed on pp. 10-14).

La Sergenté (The 'Beehive Hut')   56094863

No. 12 bus via Corbière to Petit Port, or 12a to La Pulente. The site is on open ground immediately to the west of the housing estate on the landward side of L'Oeillière Point.

It is now generally agreed that this site was wrongly interpreted by its excavators in 1923 as a dwelling, and is, in fact, a tomb of interesting form.

The structure was originally enclosed in a circular barrow of which one side has now been cut away by a cultivation terrace. The remains of the mound are now about 15m. in diameter and 1.5m. high. The circular chamber is 3.5m. in diameter with neat dry-stone walls and a paved floor. Two uprights and a sill form a doorway 0.76m. wide from a straight-sided passage at present about 2.25m. long, walled with upright slabs some 0.75m. high, and evidently preceded by a splayed or funnel-shaped entrance, probably unwalled, as in the megalithic tomb at Beauport (p. 70).

The walls of the chamber stand to some 0.75m. high, and show clear signs of corbelling, the fallen slabs having been found inside the walls. The excavators estimated its height as 'between 4 and 5 feet'. The stone is a fine pinkish granite from Mount Fiquet, about a mile away.

The only internal feature was an unpaved area about 1.5m. long at the western side of the chamber, delimited by a curved line of low uprights. To the excavators it represented a bed. Close to it, in a cavity in the floor, was a round-bottomed pot, three others being found elsewhere in the chamber, with unworked flint flakes and fragments of charcoal. No signs of burial were noted.

This tomb, owned by the Société and recently tidied up, is unique in the Islands, although the type is common enough in France, and could well mark the beginning of the passage-grave tradition in the Channel Islands.

Publication: Nicolle (1924).

La Pulente, unnamed stone   56704895

No. 12 or 12a bus to La Moye and walk up La Pulente Hill (B35) on to the golf course. The stone is at the south-west edge of the course.

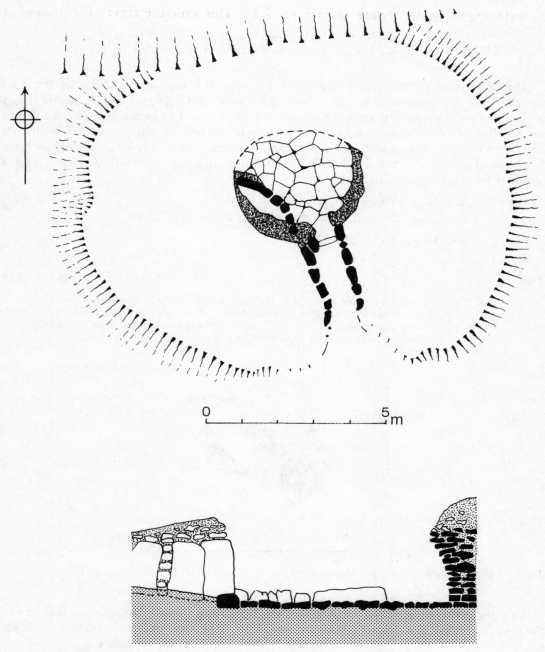

Fig. 32.   La Sergenté (source: Nicolle 1924). The section is schematic and not to scale.

This flat slab of granite (?) with one vertical side and a pointed top stands about 1.75m. above ground. It is unpublished, and has never been archaeologically investigated; however, its existence is hard to explain other than as a menhir.

About 150m. to the north-west a group of rocks is marked on the map as an antiquity, but more probably represents an exposed outcrop.

> No. 12 bus to Corbière. Walk back along the road for about 125m. and turn left
> along the old railway line, now a public footpath. The stone is a further 125m.
> along.

This large slab of red granite once lay between the two sets of lines at the now
vanished railway station. It is 3.8m. long, 2m. wide, and 0.76m. thick. It has not been
archaeologically examined since 1850, when it was found to be supported at each end
on a pillar of piled stones and earth. This crude excavation also produced fragments
of coarse pottery, burnt stones, cinders, and broken stone axes, all of which are lost.
In view of the finds and its dominating position we can reasonably regard it as a
survivor from a lost megalithic structure.

It probably owes its name (The Witnesses' Table?) to the known custom of signing
important contracts at the slab. It is certainly not a sacrificial altar.

Publication: Ahier (1852), 34.

The Ossuary   57174998

> No. 12a bus along La Grande Route des Mielles to Le Braye and the prisoner-of-war
> camp site. This structure and The Broken Menhir stand on rising ground some
> 500m. to the east of the junction with the road to the airport. Vandals have daubed
> some with paint, but otherwise their condition is much as in Rybot (1934).

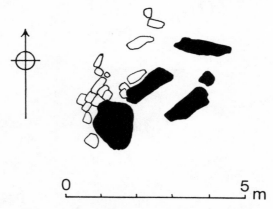

0   5 m

Fig. 33. The Ossuary (source: Darrell Hill 1924).

This inconspicuous group of stones, now becoming slightly overgrown, was found
on excavation by the Société Jersiaise in 1922 to be the ruins of a small megalithic
chamber. They re-erected one upright and conjecturally replaced a capstone;
However, the site has evidently been vandalised since then, and the remains do not now
correspond with their plan. We must therefore accept their dimensions for the
chamber as being, internally, 1.8m. by 7.6m. and 0.9m. high. They recorded a low
mound 9m. in diameter. Numerous small blocks were also found, which with several
sherds of a Jersey Bowl outside the chamber must be the result of deliberate
destruction, probably stone-robbing. All the material was granite, except for two small
blocks of shale. Three of the uprights were *in situ*, being sunk to 0.25m. into the old
land surface but not trigged.

The site was christened 'The Ossuary' from the mass of jumbled and crushed human remains. These represented at least 20 individuals, of whom the cranial and long bones predominated, the smaller bones being comparatively rare. The excavators interpreted this as evidence for the collective burial of bones cleaned by exposure—the practice of 'scarnification' evidenced elsewhere in the Channel Islands in passage-graves, for instance at Le Déhus and La Varde in Guernsey. Sir Arthur Keith, however, who examined the bones, attributed the absence of small bones to natural decay and the disturbance of the others to the process of inserting fresh burials over a period of time, and to the normal pressure of soil and sand after the collapse of the chamber. The pottery included two crude Jersey Bowls, one almost complete, with flint scrapers and flakes, and two broken 'anvil stones'.

Publication: Darrell Hill (1924).

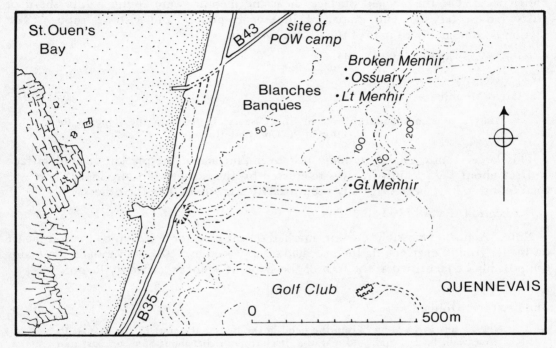

Fig. 34. Sites on the Blanches Banques. Contours in feet above sea-level. (*Crown copyright reserved*)

The Broken Menhir   57155002

Directions as above. The stone stands 30m. to the north of The Ossuary.

The odd profile of this stone, with a bite out of one side, is due to damage in antiquity and modern restoration. Discovery and excavation in 1922 proved that the broken base, set in a shallow scoop and supported by the usual trig stones, was accompanied by a second large fragment. The recognition of the 'ancient land surface' is important: it shows that the damage occurred early, as little or no blown sand had accumulated, and it demonstrates conclusively how shallow the settings of the menhirs normally were.

Restoration in 1922 used a dowel pin and a buttress of stone. Of the base, only the tip is visible today, on the seaward side; the other small block is modern.

Publication: Rybot (1934), 341-3.

The Little Menhir   57124992

Directions as above. The stone stands some 75m. to the south-west of The Ossuary.

This granite menhir has a total height of 2.3m., of which about 0.6m. is below the modern surface. Excavation in 1921 identified the ancient land surface, into which the stone was set in a shallow scoop and supported by trig stones, of which one was of mudstone and the rest of granite. The ancient subsoil was itself of blown sand, to an unknown depth, the underlying dark brown sand merging upwards into lighter blown sand. On the ancient surface, near the menhir, were found a tiny sherd of gritty red pottery, an end-scraper of flint beach-pebble, and a stone 'rubber'. The section is comparable to that of the Broken Menhir.

Publication: Rybot (1934), 341.

The Great Menhir   57174957

The stone stands about 350m. of The Ossuary, halfway up the slope in the direction of the Golf Club House.

This large granite block, standing just over 2m. above the present ground surface and set about 0.75m. into it, was re-erected by the Société Jersiaise in 1922. It was then found to have been originally supported by trig stones, like the others.

Publication: Rybot (1934), 338-9.

Note.—A further possible menhir, marked on the map some 325m. to the south-east on higher ground overlooking the rest, had disappeared by 1924. Its vandalised remains can possibly be identified at the foot of the slope. It is not recorded by Rybot.

The Beauport Dolmen   57324788

No. 12 bus at La Moye. From the bend in the B83 at the start of the lane to La Moye walk back 125m. and take the first turning right; about 35m. on, just past a road junction, is a private lane leading south; the site is to the south of the position marked on the map and is at the edge of the lawn of a house where permission should be asked.

This ruined dolmen, in a scenic position on the cliff top above Fiquet Bay, was already badly ruined when first investigated in 1877 for the Société Jersiaise. A peculiar problem of this site is that the granite bedrock splits into blocks that resemble paving and orthostats *in situ,* making the 1877 plan virtually unintelligible. Hawkes (1939, 275) thought that 'the original form of this tomb must always remain doubtful', but in 1970 a training excavation by the Société and Southampton University succeeded in recovering much of it with reasonable certainty.

It proved to be a partly megalithic, parallel-sided and undifferentiated, passage-grave, about 6m. long in a circular cairn of small granite blocks, shown schematically in Fig. 35. The edges of the cairn curved inwards to the passage entrance, which was

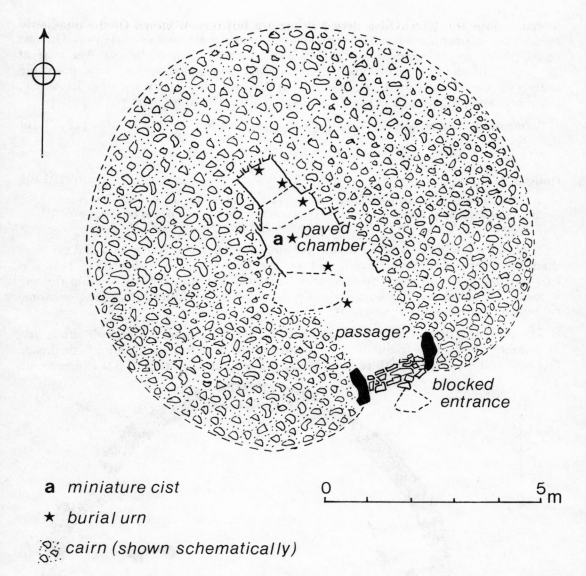

a *miniature cist*

★ *burial urn*

cairn (shown schematically)

Fig. 35.   The Beauport Dolmen (source: Johnston 1972).

marked by a pair of uprights. The passage and chamber were paved, and had been quarried into the slope at the northern end, taking advantage of the natural lines of fracture in the rock. The walls thus formed were of the natural rock to about 0.40m., the quarried material used to heighten this wall before the capstones were set in place. Another 0.40m. of wall would have been required to raise the chamber roof to that estimated for the passage (from the entrance uprights). This technique is unparalleled in the Channel Islands, but may not be significant; it may have been suggested by the appearance of the exposed rock, and in Guernsey Kendrick (1928, 107) noted something similar at La Varde.

The tomb evidently had a long history of burials and re-use. The paving is thought to be a primary feature, while the covering of sea-pebbles may be secondary. A later insertion into the paved floor was a miniature cist, consisting of four 'slab shaped stones' and a possible cover slab nearby, containing a stylistically late pot. The last vessel placed in the tomb was probably a coarse heavy urn of Bronze Age type at the mouth of the chamber. Finally, the entrance was sealed up with neat dry-stone walling—a rare feature best recorded at La Hougue Bie, Jersey (p. 65), La Varde, Guernsey, and probably also at Les Pourciaux North, Alderney.

Publication: Cable (1877) for the earlier excavation, and Johnston (1972) for the later.

Hougue de Vinde   60704705

> No. 17 bus to Woodbines Corner (or No. 16 to Portelet Corner, but with a longer walk). Take the lane to Noirmont Headland, and the site is visible as an overgrown mound in bracken to the left of the road to Portelet from the Public Works Depot.

This was a low mound of earth and rubble some 15–18m. in diameter and no more than 1m. high when first investigated by the Société Jersiaise in 1881. This was followed by more thorough re-excavation in 1913. Now in public ownership the site is badly neglected and has been seriously damaged by unauthorised digging or stone-robbing in relatively recent years.

The principal discovery in both excavations was a circular rubble wall about 9m. in diameter, built on a foundation of weather-worn boulders and 1.06m. high. Inside this wall and concentric with it were found the remains of a ring of flat stones set on

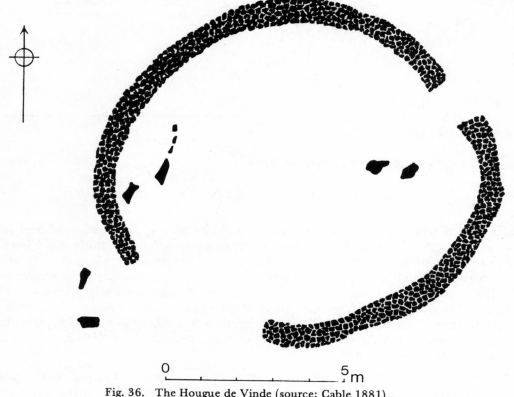

0   5 m

Fig. 36.   The Hougue de Vinde (source: Cable 1881).

edge, forming a circle just over 6.7m. in diameter. These slabs were up to 1m. high and had once possessed a 'well fitted rubble coping' of which parts were found in place. The destruction of this, and two opposing gaps in the wall, were probably the work of treasure-seekers of the 16th century—to judge from medieval pottery and other datable finds.

Prehistoric finds were scanty, consisting of stone rubbers and polishers and worked flints including a possible arrow-head (now lost). Several displaced blocks inside the circle were not thought to be from a cist, and no human remains were recorded. Nevertheless, in view of the finds and the extensive ransacking of the site, this can be ranked with Les Cinq Pierres and Les Platons as one of the late- or post-megalithic burial mounds discussed on p. 33.

Publications: Cable (1881) for the first investigation, and Marrett (1913) for the later.

PARISH OF ST. CLEMENT

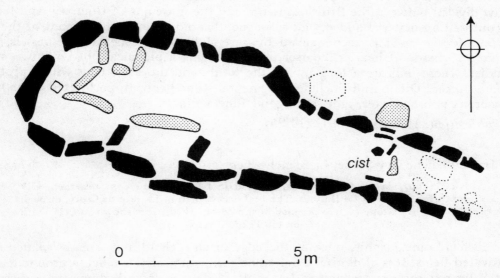

Fig. 37.   Le Mont Ubé (source: Hawkes 1939). The position of stones destroyed between 1848 and 1921 is shown stippled.

Mont Ubé   67694742

No. 1a bus via St. Clements Inner Road to La Blinderie crossroads. Walk north about 225m., and the monument is inconspicuously sign-posted on a stone marker at the right of the road. Approach the site by this woodland path, not by the private drive which leads to a house. The site is owned by the Société Jersiaise and is surrounded by a tall hedge.

This fine passage-grave was discovered in 1848 by workmen quarrying building stone, who had already blasted all the capstones before W. C. Lukis managed to save the rest. At this time it served as a pigsty, and since its discovery has suffered further mutilations.

The chamber and passage were originally covered by a mound, which Lukis recorded. A peristalith of upright stones (now vanished) is also probable. It is of

73

the bottle-shaped, undifferentiated form usual in the Channel Islands, the chamber measuring about 7.3m. by 3m., approached by 5m. of passage tapering from 1.16m. at its present entrance to 1.8m. at the junction with the chamber. No capstones remain in place. It is likely that the floor was paved with slabs, of which no trace now survives. An unusual feature that does survive is a shallow internal side-chamber on the south, framed by two tall uprights, 1.5m. and 1.8m. high, its depth slightly increased by the device of setting one of the uprights of the southern wall behind the rest. There were originally at least two of these, perhaps four; their position is shown dotted on the plan. A drawing by Lukis shows that these chambers were closed by low rectangular slabs. This recalls the series of internal chambers in the circular tomb of Mont de la Ville, Fort Regent (p. 28), and possibly La Pouquelaye de Faldouet (pp. 81-3) in its present much-restored form.

In the passage are three small uprights, while a fourth lies fallen between them. These once formed a small cist, or miniature 'dolmen', with a capstone; no finds from this are recorded.

The finds include 10–12 pots recovered in fragments by Lukis, but the collection (now divided between the British Museum and the museums of Guernsey and Jersey) is confused by material added, and subsequently sold, by a former tenant of the site. A fine Jersey Bowl is accompanied by several beakers or beaker-like vessels, with numerous sherds of heavier, coarser urns, including a biconical pot with two strap-handles. These indicate a long use of the tomb, and the series ends with a probable Roman piece. Other finds include a segmental stone pendant, perforated stone rings, numerous polished axes, and some good flint artifacts.

Publication: Hawkes (1939), 214-25).

La Dame Blanche (Ivy Stone, La Blanche Pierre) 67724683

> No. 1a bus via St. Clements Inner Road to La Blinderie crossroads, then walk south for 200m. to Le Haguais. The best access is from La Rue de Croix, through the farm Ivy Stone (where permission should be asked). It is shown too far south on the 1:2,500 map.

This handsome menhir, once at the edge of an orchard, now stands isolated amid cultivated fields. It is of diorite, 2.5m. in height, with nearly 1m. below ground,making it the longest surviving menhir in Jersey. Its surface is unworked, except perhaps for the pointed tip which may have been artificially smoothed (or, according to one theory 'vitrification by lightning'). When the orchard was dug up in 1934 a shallow, stone-lined depression packed with limpets was found 3.6m. to the south-west, prompting an excavation by the Société Jersiaise of the menhir. This proved to be set in an oval pit, 0.5m. deep and supported by small trig stones (Fig. 16a).

Publication: Rybot (1934), 337–8.

Green Island (La Motte) 6745

> No. 1a bus to Green Island. The island is accessible only at low tide.

Green island was a promontory in prehistoric times, and probably until the beginning of the 17th century A.D. It deserves its name, as it has preserved some of its topsoil and grass, in spite of erosion. It was this erosion that, in 1911, exposed the first of a series of burial cists that were subsequently excavated by the Société Jersiaise. There were at least 15 of them, rectangular boxes made of slabs of the Island diorite, roofed with capstones. They were tidily set out as a cemetery, orientated east-west. Some were long enough to take an extended burial, only one being wide enough for a crouched burial, as was indeed the case. The small ones could have been receptacles for scarnified bones, but gradations of size suggested to the excavators that they had been for children. Most contained fragmentary bones, and in only four did determinable skeletal material survive. One was in a crouched posture, another a double burial, adult and child.

A large cairn of diorite boulders was found to cover most of the east end of the island, and this was inconclusively trenched. A quantity of bone detritus in the centre suggests that it may also have been funerary.

Settlement evidence in the form of midden deposits of charcoal, animal bone, pottery and shells was found in the trench across the cairn, and at intervals along the north coast of the island, with one outlier on the south. The excavation established that the middens overlay the edge of the cairn, and therefore post-dated it, but were covered by the same deposit of blown sand.

The finds span a long period, from a shallow vase-support (the only one from a domestic context) and sherds of six Jersey Bowls, through coarser urns (one with a lug handle), to a grooved sherd of Iron Age date. The stone rubbers and hammer-stones and some flint flakes were unhelpful, and the relationship of settlement to cemetery remains unclear.

Today, only hollows mark the site of the cists, which have been reconstructed at the museum at La Hougue Bie. Natural and human erosion is fast reducing the surviving vegetation, and the loss of the archaeological levels is a matter of concern.

The site can be paralleled in Brittany, in the Early and Middle Bronze Ages.

Publication: Nicolle and Sinel (1912–14) record the excavations: *see also* Marrett (1912), 209. For recent finds, *see Annu. Bull. Soc. Jersiaise* 22, 1980, 372-373.

PARISH OF ST. HELIER

Note.—For the displaced monument of Mont de la Ville and for the gas works site, see pp. 28, 63. Some stones of the avenue of the latter have been moved to the museum of La Hougue Bie.

Ville-ès-Nouaux   63453989

Nos. 6, 7, 8, 9, 9a, 12, 12a, 14, 15, 16 and 17 buses to First Tower. The sites are within railings, in the park by St. Andrew's church.

Two monuments, a gallery-grave and a cist with stone circle, are preserved. In addition, a cinerary urn, a cairn and two further cists were also found. The cairn (A on Fig. 38) was of rubble and earth, a cist is shown at B, and another at C. This last was 1.8m. from the circle, and was 2.4m. long and formed of five stones. It was embedded in the sand at a depth of 0.2m. below its upper surface, and stood on a bed of ash and burnt earth. Nothing was found inside it except ashes and earth, but there were some fragments of pottery within 0.6m. of it.

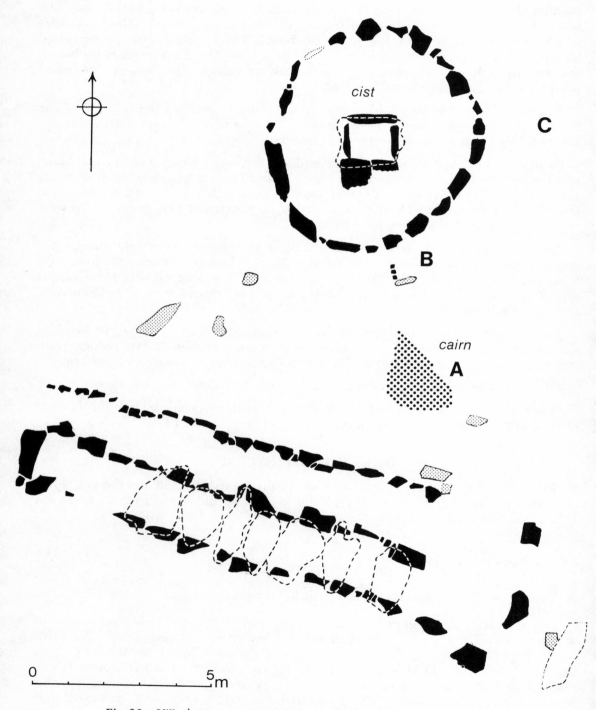

Fig. 38. Ville-ès-Nouaux, gallery-grave, cist etc. (source: Hawkes 1939).

The gallery-grave is important for the rarity of this class of monument in the Islands, and the two excavations of 1879 and 1883 leave much to be desired. The identification as a gallery-grave is suggested by the row of stones parallel with the north wall of the tomb, a kerb with rubble packing behind it. On the other hand the excavators, who were no doubt expecting a passage-grave, thought they saw a cruciform arrangement of chambers at the ruined eastern end. There is no doubt, however, that the tomb had a long mound or cairn, in contrast to the circular mounds of the passage-graves. Three levels of burials were identified, two floor levels in the galley, one 0.2m. above the other, and the layer of blown sand over the site. The lower floor produced only limpets and rough pottery (now lost) on a pavement of beach-pebbles. The upper floor contained about a dozen Bell-beakers (nine of them fairly complete) and beaker-type pottery with one of the two archer's wrist-guards from Jersey, but no limpets. The beakers were protected by flat stones placed around and above them so as to form tiny cists. At a much higher level, in the blown sand, was a heap of ashes and further interments, an inverted urn of the Breton ribbon-handled type, and other urns, mostly of Iron Age type. Two or three urns had been protected by slabs.

The second tomb, intact but empty on discovery, was a slab-lined cist 1.2m. by 1.0m. internally, with a rectangular capstone. The kerb was a slightly flattened circle, about 4.2m. in diameter, of upright slabs varying greatly in size. The rubble packed inside these suggests a cairn over a bell-shaped core of 'clay' resembling the loess core of the Tourgis Dolmen, Alderney, also a cist (p. 129).

Publication: Hawkes (1939), 259-269.

PARISH OF ST. JOHN

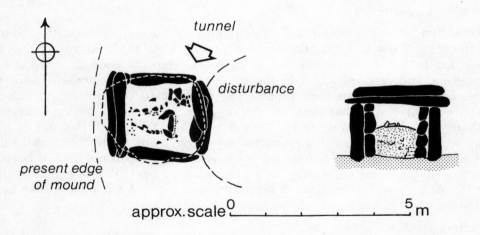

Fig. 39. La Hougue Boëte (source: Hawkes 1939 with additions). The section shows the west end of the cist.

La Hougue Boëte   62425477

Nos. 5 and 6 bus to St. John's church. A lane leads south-west for about 700m. where the tree-covered mound stands on the right-hand side at a bend.

La Hougue Boëte owes its steep profile and triangular shape partly to the stability of the loess composing it, partly to mutilation by the lane on one side and cultivation on the other two. It stands 4.5m. high.

A cavity at the top was made in about 1970 by children, not by the original excavators of 1911, who tunnelled from the north-east side in their desire not to spoil the exterior of the mound. The disturbance has enabled a partial inspection to be made of the interior. This broadly confirms the original plan while casting doubt on the dimensions; the re-examination gives the internal dimensions as about 3.6m. by 1.3m. with the capstone of roughly the same size. The four main slabs forming the walls seem to have been originally surmounted by two long ones at the east end and a 'lintel' spanning the full width of the west end; these stones, and smaller ones at various points around the circumference were to provide a level base for the capstone. Additional support is supposed to have been provided at the west end—and here the original plan and section part company—by two pillars of smaller blocks (Fig. 39). Three blocks forming such a pillar have been observed at the north-east corner of the chamber, but none elsewhere.

The chamber is now so silted up that there is no sign of the internal structures recorded in 1911, and indeed they may have been removed in the search for a burial beneath them. They have the appearance of a roughly-built cist, and the larger end stones sealed the leg bones of a bird. Below this, and halfway down the deposit, was a remarkable main burial: a horse with its head supported on a pile of stones, and a man with his head resting on the horse's neck, accompanied by a 'round-bottomed vessel' of dark gritty ware, a fragment of a greenstone axe and a curious flint implement with a narrow grip expanding into a terminal disc. None of these finds can now be identified, and the only pottery bases preserved are wheel-turned vessels of late Iron Age or Gallo-Roman date. The horse's teeth have recently been found to be modern, and considerable doubt is now felt about the details of the original description of the burial.

The condition of this monument is undoubtedly deteriorating; truncation of the sides of the mound has brought the chamber very close to the western edge, and a rabbit-hole has linked the two. The pit, some 2.4m. deep, exposed the eastern end of the capstone and revealed a gap in the stonework at this end—perhaps made by the excavators on entry from their tunnel. The entrance to this tunnel can be seen from the roadside, of fine but derelict masonry, the tunnel itself having collapsed. Most seriously, the north and south walls are now known to have shifted out of true under the weight of the capstone, estimated to weigh about twelve tons. Estimates prepared in 1972 for the excavation and consolidation of this tomb proved beyond the resources of the Société Jersiaise; it was accordingly backfilled in the hope that one day it will be possible to make a proper investigation of what must have been a quite unusual monument.

Publication: Hawkes (1939), 250-3.

Frémont Point   63885613

No. 5 bus to Bonne Nuit Bay.

A faint earthwork cutting off the promontory can be made out. Incomplete excavations in 1963 showed that it consisted of a single bank and ditch, with the

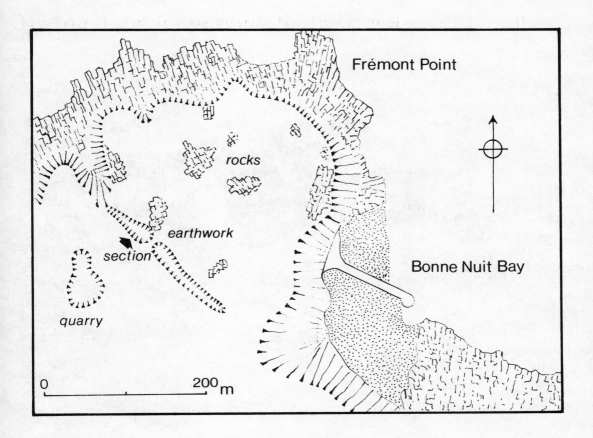

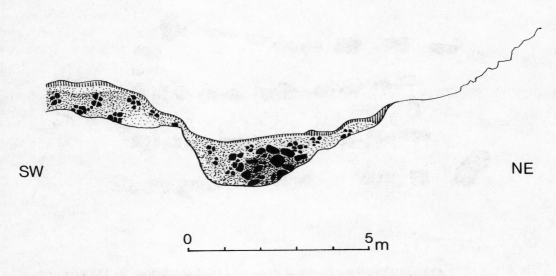

Fig. 40.   Promontory fort, Frémont Point (source: Willy, 1964).

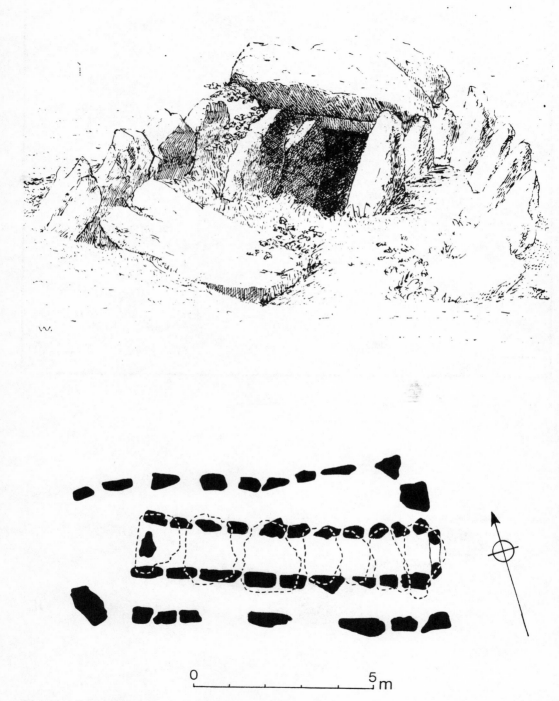

Fig. 41.   Gallery-grave, Le Couperon. Above, drawing by F. C. Lukis before the 1868 restoration: below: after the 1919 work (source: Hawkes 1939).

upcast apparently spread in front as a glacis. No timber lacing or palisade was detected, but the inner side of the ditch was possibly surmounted by a wall revetting the face of the bank. The possible position of this can be seen in the section (Fig. 40) on the south-west lip of the ditch; the stones in the ditch are interpreted as the tumble from this revetment. Numerous beach-pebbles of standard sizes were interpreted as possible sling-stones. Air-photographs have subsequently identified two phases, and this has been confirmed by ground survey.

Publication: Willy (1964); *see also Annu. Bull. Soc. Jersiaise* 22, 1979, 247.

PARISH OF ST. MARTIN

Le Couperon   70345416

> No. 3 or 3b bus to Rouzel Bay. The dolmen stands on a promontory about 750m.
> due east of Rozel. On foot, follow the B38 for about 900m. until a winding path on
> the left leads to the site. Access by car is from the B91 along a steep and winding
> lane.

Scenically, this gallery-grave must be one of Jersey's most attractive monuments, though what we see is largely restoration. Fortunately, the ruins were recorded by W. C. Lukis before the operations of 1868, showing that the effect of restoration, if not the actual position of stones, is broadly correct. Some useful adjustments were made in 1919.

The long mound that covered the tomb is reliably recorded, although undetectable today. The kerb of this survives as the 18 stones of the outer ring. Today the eastern end of the chamber is flush with the outer ring; Lukis's plan, however, suggests that the kerb may have been continuous here, with the chamber fully enclosed by the mound a little distance inside it. Certainly, the slab with a bite out of it that closes the east end is wrong; it is half a slab, or one of a pair, forming a 'kennel-hole' and its proper position, on Continental analogies, would have been as a divider halfway along the gallery. The first restoration used it as a capstone, and it was moved in 1919 to its present position in the realisation that it would no longer fit the tomb in its restored form.

Some pottery was found, and some allegedly Iron Age material; none is described in detail, and all are now lost.

Publication: Hawkes (1939), 254-8.

La Pouquelaye de Faldouet   70995069

> Nos. 1 or 1s bus to Gorey Pier. Walk back along the B28 a short distance to where
> the B29 forks right towards Petit Portelet Bay. Take this road for 100m. and take
> the first turning left which leads steeply up the hill. At the top, 300m. on, take the
> turning on the right opposite some houses; almost immediately turn left and follow
> this road for another 250m. The entrance to the site is just beyond the fork, on
> the left, and lies at the end of a tree-lined path.

This baffling site, which has been much mauled by diggers and restorers who were not archaeologists, is now owned and well maintained by the Société Jersiaise. A passage of 17 stones, slightly bow-sided on the north, and 5m. long, leads to a roughly circular chamber surrounded by four chambers (out of a possible eight).

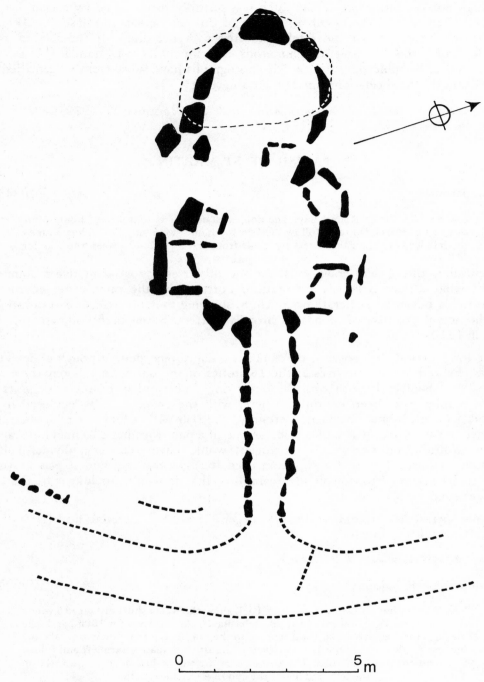

Fig. 42. La Pouquelaye de Faldouet (source: Rybot 1932).

Beyond that is a further horseshoe chamber, of seven large uprights covered by a huge capstone whose weight is estimated at 23–4 tons.

This chamber is the only part of the monument we can trust, as sheer size will have preserved it from 'restoration'. In 1839 it was the only part protruding from a large mound, when clearance of the site was begun; digging and rebuilding of the rest was complete by 1868. The eastern edge of the mound was found to cover two dry-stone retaining walls, and fragments perhaps of two more. These were rebuilt to give the funnel-shaped entrance that we see today, but re-excavation by the Société in 1910 showed that the outer one, at least, was originally unbroken, and that it probably, but not certainly, encircled the mound. The most extensive restoration was of the ring of chambers, particularly those on the south side; fortunately W. C. Lukis was able to plan the terminal chamber and the two immediately adjoining it on the north-east, showing that these, at least, are authentic and contained human remains. We can only hope that the reconstruction of the rest was based on sound evidence. A coloured plan of 1873, preserved in the Library of the Society of Antiquaries, London (Red Portfolio BP 58) purports to show stones recently and doubtfully replaced.

A structure of such peculiar form demands an explanation, and a reasonable hypothesis is this: the horseshoe-shaped terminal chamber and (possibly) the passage are the survivors of a straightfoward passage-grave. Subsequently, the western end (at least) of the passage was dug out and removed to make way for a second passage-grave like that of Le Mont de la Ville (p. 28). Bearing in mind the size of the mound, the logistics of this may seem daunting; but much of the material for the new structure was now to hand, and the 6m.-wide trench required would have proved easier than building a new tomb elsewhere. The rebuilding of chambered tombs is now well attested in France and the British Isles, though hitherto not recorded in the Channel Isles. A comparable history of modification is proposed for the Sandy Hook dolmen, in Guernsey (p. 99), and there may be other unrecognised instances elsewhere in the Islands.

The finds were copious and well preserved, and all or most have survived—except the human remains which were re-buried. At least three skeletons (two male and one female) with children's bones are recorded; one skeleton is said to have been in a sitting posture—an unusual feature paralleled elsewhere (p. 84). Unfortunately, the find-spots of the pottery, stone axes and flints were not recorded, so they cannot be used to test the two-period hypothesis. Interestingly, two round-bottomed pots are said to have been found in position on the saucer-shaped 'vase-supports'.

Publication: the literature is collated and the finds published in Rybot (1932) and Hawkes (1939), 229-238; for the reinterpretation, *see* Johnston (1977 b), 53-4.

Ile Agois   59615569

No. 6 bus to St. Mary's church, and walk northwards from the crossroads, using a map, until the cliffs are reached. Find the deepest and most southerly point of the Crabbé inlet and descend the cleft where the stream goes down. (Note that there is another stream descending a sheer cliff further N.E.). The island is accessible only at low tide by this scramble down to the rocks and an equally stiff climb on the other side.

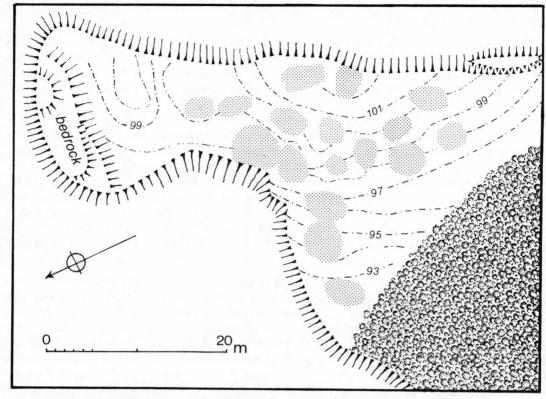

Fig. 43. Habitation sites on the Ile Agois (source: Finlaison and Holdsworth 1979).
Contours at 2m. intervals.

The hollows on the sloping side of this rock mark the sites of several circular, earth-embanked huts, and at the summit, three built of stone. Crowning the rock was a rectangular structure. They were excavated by the Société Jersiaise in 1974–5. The evidence for believing that this represented a small community of hermit monks with their chapel is discussed on p. 53.

Publication: Finlaison and Holdsworth (1979).

PARISH OF ST. OUEN

Dolmen des Monts Grantez   56685368

No. 9 or 9a bus to St. Ouen's Manor crossroads, about 2km. from the site. Sometimes the No. 9 goes to St. Ouen's church, which shortens the walk by some 10 minutes. From the crossroads take the road to St. Ouen's church, branching right in about 250 m. towards Ville au Bas. At the crossroads here turn right on the road to St. Anne's church. Half a kilometre along is Les Hanières, with its conspicuous greenhouses; ignore the road forking right and just beyond it turn off left along the Val es Roues. Another 10 minutes' walk will bring you to the dolmen signposted through the fields to the left.

The excavation of this fine passage-grave in 1912 gave the Société Jersiaise an opportunity to investigate a largely undisturbed tomb; the side-chamber had been ransacked, the cracked capstone being supported on a pile of granite slabs, and there was a gap in the south wall of the tomb, opposite the side-chamber. So, since the whole was invisible under its mound, we may suppose that it had been entered by tunnelling or trenching from the south; and that the stratification and finds of the passage and main chamber were still intact in 1912.

The mound, in contrast to the little we know of others in the Channel Islands, was not a true, but a flattened circle, 18m. by 6m. The internal structure is now completely exposed, showing a bottle-shaped, or undifferentiated, passage-grave 9.7m. long, with a single side-chamber. The main chamber is now unroofed, but most of the other capstones are in place; that over the side-chamber was repaired in 1931. Most of the dry-stone walling between the uprights is modern, but presumably faithful to its original, though the gap in the south wall may have formerly been filled by an upright. The stratification did not show the superimposed levels noted elsewhere; it consisted simply of a floor of yellow clay, overlaid by nearly a metre of black soil with an infiltration of rubble from the mound, and 0.3m. of sand in contact with the capstones.

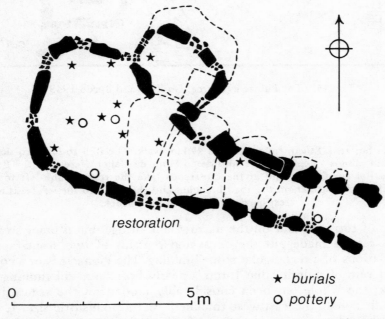

Fig. 44. Dolmen de Monts Grantez (source: Hawkes 1939).

No intact burials are recorded from the side-chamber, simply a few loose bones, and a shallow, round-bottomed pottery saucer with a pair of perforations just below the rim. The main chamber contained seven crouched burials, six adults and one child (asterisked on Fig. 44), as well as a loose mandible, skull fragments, and teeth of a possible eighth. The burials were accompanied by pottery, quantities of limpet shells, bones and teeth of ox, deer, horse, pig and goat, and selected pretty pebbles. At the northern junction of passage and chamber was a seated skeleton, with its back against the wall, like a sentry asleep at his post. A fragment of a carinated bowl was found in the passage, beneath the eastern-most capstone.

Publication: Hawkes (1939), 208-213.

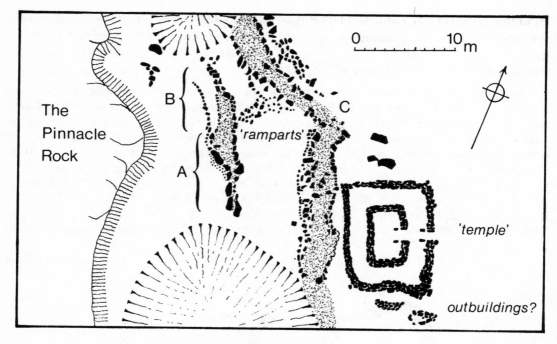

Fig. 45. The Pinnacle (source: Godfray and Burdo 1949).

The Pinnacle

54495547

No. 12a bus to L'Etacq, followed by a 4½km. walk. The B35 to le Puleq doubles back and climbs steeply up the hillside to Mont du Vallet. Here take the B55 to Ville la Bas for 600m., and at the crossroads take the road to the left towards the cliffs. 25m. further on the road branches and the track to the left leads to the crest overlooking the Pinnacle Rock.

At the base of the rock and on the narrow land-bridge that is being steadily eroded on both sides can be made out the excavated remains of two stone-faced ramparts and the foundations of a rectangular stone building. The Pinnacle is of a coarse-grained granite with a vein of dolerite that forms a nearly horizontal sill running underneath the main rock; the whole has been considerably eroded on the seaward side and is probably less than half the east-west thickness of its prehistoric size. It is separated from the mainland by a sea-worn gulley of which the upper part is firmly blocked by head except at one place where it has collapsed. This must have been stable for thousands of years as it runs underneath the ramparts. It is also important to remember that more than half the occupied site has also probably fallen away since prehistoric times. Some 400m. to the north-east is a good freshwater spring with a deeply-cut stream—the Canal du Squez—that enters the sea with a miniature waterfall close to the site. This may have influenced the choice of site for settlement, and traces can still be detected of a path connecting the two.

Excavations by the Société Jersiaise between 1930 and 1936 showed that the first occupation was early in the neolithic period, with a radiocarbon date of 3070 ± 100 B.C. This occupation belongs to the southern, thicker, part of the inner 'rampart' (A) which was of earth and rubble with a stone facing. This was interpreted as a retaining wall for an earthen platform or terrace against the base of the rock. No dwellings were found, but seven hearths and dumps of uncertain material preceded the supposed platform.

A clear turf line separated this from the next occupation, a transitional phase from neolithic to Bronze Age, characterised by two artifacts (a bead and a flat axe) of copper (not bronze), bell-beakers and barbed-and-tanged arrowheads. To this phase belongs the northern part of the inner 'rampart' (B) which seems to have been a rebuilding of the platform. The stones were smaller, the workmanship inferior, and a mass of stones was added on the outside to prevent collapse.

Occupation was now continuous into the Bronze Age, when the outermost 'rampart' (C) was added. Earth and rubble were quarried from behind it, the resulting bank being faced by large upright slabs set on edge. Sparse finds and lack of dwellings suggested that this was not an occupied site, but a refuge, the find of carbonised beans being interpreted as a 'food store'.

Occupation in the Iron Age is attested by six pieces of iron and another find of the first century B.C., but no structures.

Finally, the Roman period is marked by the rectangular building, whose excavated foundations have suffered from the same vandalism that has rolled much of the other stonework over the cliff-edge since the excavation. The prehistoric ramparts themselves were apparently demolished to provide material for the two concentric walls of what must be a Gallo-Roman temple. It is not the normal square, but an oblong measuring 11.20m. by 9.15m. externally; the likely appearance of the superstructure is discussed above (p. 50 and Fig. 28); we must add what were thought to be the fragmentary remains of three further structures (lean-tos or outbuildings) at the south and south-east. Finds were sparse, but included a coin of Commodus (A.D. 180–191). The interpretation as a temple is supported by the proximity of the spring, but weakened by the absence of religious objects and of the usually copious small dedicatory offerings, including coins.

The structural sequence given here is reasonably secure, though some of the excavators' other interpretations are open to question. In particular, the neolithic phase may represent not a conventional settlement but a specialised axe-making factory exploiting the vein of dolerite in the Pinnacle Rock.

The structures were restored by the Société Jersiaise, but have since been vandalised both by treasure-seekers and by thoughtless visitors. Readers are asked to help the Société in its task of maintaining this important site.

Publication: Godfray and Burdo (1949–50); for the axe-factory *see* Renouf and Urry (1976, 82–3), and for the radiocarbon date *Annu. Bull. Soc. Jersiaise* 20, 1969. 12.

Hougue de Grosnez   55165653

No. 9a bus to Grosnez. Leave the track to the castle after about 400m. and strike
northwards towards the cliffs. Alternatively, an attractive cliff-top walk of about
2½km. from The Pinnacle passes the ruined castle.

Today the site is an inconspicuous low mound in broken terrain with many small paths. It survived to about 1m. high before excavation in 1923, and was about 15m. in diameter. The centre had been devastated, and only three granite boulders of a megalithic structure survived, measuring 0.76m. to 1.22m. in length. A fourth stone, 1.06m. in length, lay in the edge of the mound. The central area had a paved floor of red soil overlain by 0.38m. of earth. The form of the structure is uncertain; but the finds, which included round-bottomed pots and a fragmentary 'vase-support', are appropriate to a large passage-grave.

Publication: Rybot (1924).

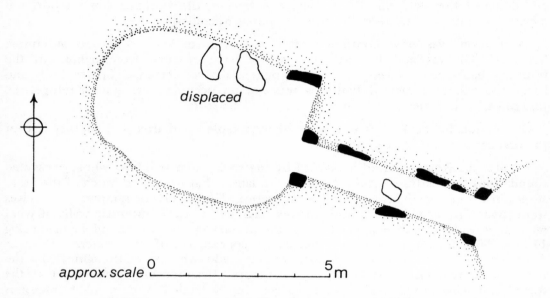

approx. scale 0 _____ 5 m

Fig. 46.   The Dolmen des Géonnais (source: Baal 1930).

Dolmen des Géonnais   57295580

No. 9 bus to Vinchelez. Take the lane leading north-east from the junction by Vinchelez Manor. The site is about 450m. along it, past the second pair of cottages and to the right of the lane.

The structure is now virtually invisible in bracken and high gorse, in which slight traces of a circular mound can be made out, with a central cavity. The relief is probably accentuated by the upcast from the 1929 excavations, which were only partly backfilled.

The site, also known as 'The Hougue', was thought to be a megalithic monument as early as 1859, though the 1929 excavations by the Société Jersiaise showed that it had been extensively damaged by quarrying—apparently for stone used in the nearby houses. All the capstones had perished and the uprights had been decapitated, displaced, or entirely removed. The only certain feature of the plan is the passage, 5½m. long, narrowing slightly towards the chamber, from 1.06m. to 0.83m. A semi-circular forecourt is suggested on the plan; this, however, would be unusual, and may be supposition. Another unusual feature is the sharp differentiation of passage from chamber, though of the latter only one stone survived *in situ*. The lop-sidedness of the plan suggests that this might easily represent a single ruined side-chamber.

88

The finds were copious, although badly crushed by the quarrymen. A fragment of human jaw was the only sign of burial, but the pottery covered a wide range of form and date, suggesting a long use for the tomb. It included a fine vase-support, large and small urns with plain lugs and finger-tipping, and a Jersey Bowl. Other finds included a pottery spindle-whorl and a pierced disc or bead of fibrous material. The absence of limpet-shells was noted.

Publication: Baal (1930).

Plémont Point 56305671

No. 9 or 9a bus to Plémont. Tracks lead past the buildings of Pontin's holiday camp to the headland.

The narrow peninsula of Plémont Point was cut by a bank and ditch which can still be made out, and are thought to be the remains of a promontory fort of Iron Age date. The site is unpublished.

PARISH OF ST. PETER

The White Menhir 57055143

No. 12a bus along La Grande Route des Mielles. From Le Port take the track north-eastwards towards La Mare Mills (not the main road to St. Peter's church). 450m. from the junction enter the fields to the left. The stone is about 75m. to the north, on the seaward side of a field boundary. It is about 20 minutes' walk from the group that comprises the Ossuary and associated menhirs (pp. 68-70).

This small but apparently unbroken menhir is 1.08m. high and 0.75m. at its widest, with less than 0.3m below the surface. It serves no purpose either as a boundary stone or as a landmark, and is of granite that must have been brought at least two miles; most important, it is supported by trig stones, as are the other menhirs.

Publication: Rybot (1934), 345

Les Trois Rocques 57075166

This group stands conspicuously in open ground 225m. north of The White Menhir.

Two squat rocks and one thin slab set some distance away and not quite in a straight line are traditionally three menhirs; investigation in 1933 suggested that they were of no great antiquity. They have been brought, presumably by man, some two miles from their source, and the tops of two seem to have been artificially shaped. On the other hand, their site is unusually low-lying, their squat shape is unorthodox, they were found not be be supported by the usual trig stones, and they are set in the more recent blown sand. The smallest was re-erected (and trigged) in 1913.

These three stones are surrounded by a low circular bank that can be faintly made out, and cup-markings have been identified on the top of one.

Publication: Rybot (1934), 343–4.

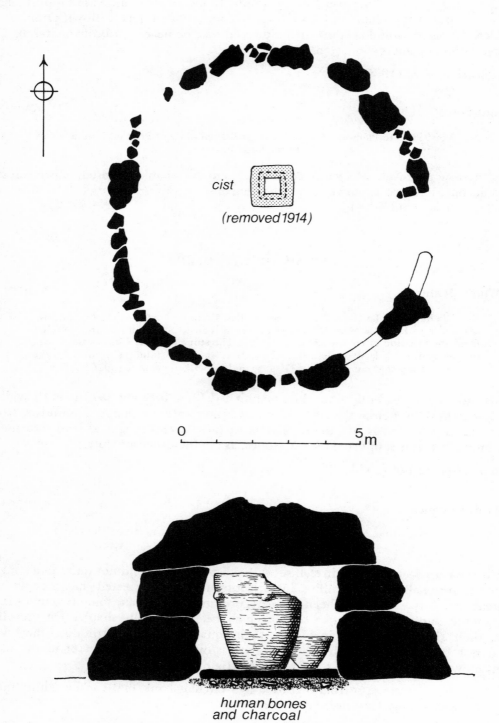

cist

(removed 1914)

0   5 m

human bones
and charcoal

Fig. 47.   The Hougue des Platons (sources: Hawkes 1939, Baal and Sinel 1915).

PARISH OF TRINITY

Hougue des Platons 65625564

No. 4 bus to Les Platons. Take the track leading north-west from Les Platons Road. The site is overgrown and hard to find, and enquiry should be made at the two houses at the end of the track.

The site was excavated twice, in 1914, and again in 1936, when it was restored (without the central cist which was removed to safety). It consists of a circular low mound, some 8.2m. in diameter, enclosed in a rough stone oval. This last consisted of rough blocks of varying size laid lengthwise, the gaps being filled with crude dry-stone walling. The mound was of fine buff clay in distinct layers, and the excavators noted an area of disturbance in the layers around the top of the cist. It is not possible to tell from the account whether this represents a later remodelling of the cist, or an abortive attempt at tomb-robbing. The recorded depression suggests the latter; at all events, the contents were intact.

The cist was about half a metre north of the true centre. The broad walls, 0.35m. high, built of flat slabs set lengthwise on each other, supported a capstone roughly 0.76m. square. The cist was paved with a single slab and enclosed two urns, the larger of which contained cremated remains. It was a late Bronze Age bucket-shaped urn, originally with four lugs and incomplete when buried. The human remains were supposed to be those of an adult (probably a woman) and a child. Below the paving were found the scattered traces of a further cremation. The cist was moved to the museum, and is now at the new museum at La Hougue Bie.

Publication: Baal and Sinel (1915 a); Hawkes (1939), 296-299.

Note.—About 750m. due east is La Roche à la Fée (66405563), a large block of conglomerate apparently supported by three pieces of the same material lying on a bare surface of conglomerate. Its possible megalithic origins have been discussed by Hawkes (1939, 312); in this case, two of the smaller stones are possible fragments of a single upright, broken when the 'structure' collapsed. The bare rock underneath makes a burial unlikely, but both this and the cliff-side situation urge comparison with the two new structures in Sark (pp. 121-4). This site is marked on the maps as 'La Pierre de la Fételle', but the alternative name is preferable to avoid confusion with a (natural) stone of the same name at 66815081.

Le Câtel 68915464

No. 3 bus to Le Câtel. At the first road fork where the road leads down the hill to Rozel Bay take the left fork and presently turn left at the T-junction. The earthwork is now on your left, and is best approached from the point where the lane makes a right-angled turn to the right. The site is on farmland, and permission must be sought at the farm.

This is one of the largest, and certainly the best preserved, of the Iron Age fortifications in the Channel Islands. Nearly 200m. of it survives to a height of 6m. with steep sides and a rounded top. It owes its steep profile to the stability of the loess of which it is constructed. A geophysical survey in 1970 failed to find a ditch, or even a scoop for this material.

91

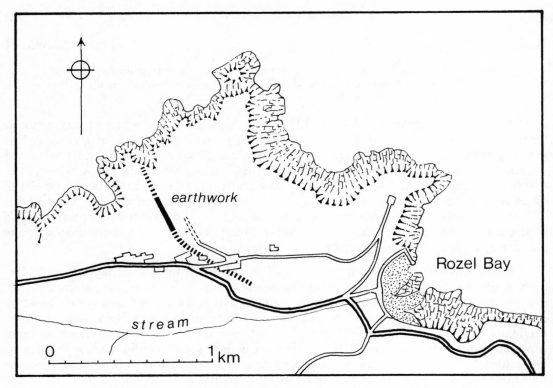

Fig. 48. Promontory fort, Le Câtel (source: Cotton 1954).

Its original length is unknown, but in 1809 it was said to be a quarter of a mile long (that is, to the modern road and perhaps beyond); it was evidently intended to cut off the tongue of high ground between Rozel Bay and Bouley Bay.

Its Iron Age date is a likely supposition, and bricks, tiles, and other Roman material allegedly found in the rampart material would suggest maintenance, at least, in the Roman period. Roman pottery is still found in the cultivated ground behind it.

Publication: Hawkes (1939), 192-3; the 1970 survey is unpublished. For an appreciation, *see* Cotton (1958).

GUERNSEY

Guernsey is the second largest of the Channel Islands, with an area of about 64 square kilometres, and is the most distant from the mainland. The gneissic rocks of most of the island are older than those of Jersey, while the gabbros of the northern part are related to those of north-west Jersey, and part of Alderney. True granites are found in the two western points of L'Erée and Pleinmont. The result is a varied coastline, with cliffs, offshore islands, and bays, great and small. The harder rocks of the southern half form a large cultivated plateau, rising towards the cliffs of the south coast, while the lower northern part terminates in the coastal plain of L'Ancresse Common.

The reasons why Guernsey, in contrast to Jersey, has no inhabited caves of the Palaeolithic period have been explained above (pp. 8-9). The evidence for mesolithic settlement is largely coastal, and here also much has been lost to marine encroachment. The eroded remains of the loess cover have encouraged neolithic and later settlement over the whole island, but the concentration of megalithic remains in the north is probably misleading. For place-names and the results of fieldwork have shown that our losses, both in settlements and in funerary monuments, have been particularly severe in the south; de Guérin (1921, 30) suggested that there had been 68 dolmens of which 15 survived, and 39 menhirs.

The Iron Age is represented by cist burials, coins, pottery, etc., two recently-excavated settlements, and the fine promontory fort at Jerbourg. Guernsey lay directly on the sea-route between north-western France and Britain, and apparently prospered until, at least, the middle of the first century B.C. However, subsequent Continental contacts, particularly with Roman Gaul, have left surprisingly little evidence in the island, though the offshore wrecks (pp. 46-7) show that these contacts were maintained.

In comparison with Jersey, there are fewer monuments and sites for the visitor, though those that have survived are impressive, and in one or two cases, unusual. The Déhus tomb, for instance, is the equal of La Hougue Bie in Jersey, not for size but for sophistication and complexity; moreover, this and the statue-menhirs bear the only neolithic art in the Channel Islands. In fieldwork and excavation the Société Guernesiaise has recently reached a peak of activity not seen in the island since the days of the Lukis family; and the transfer of the Lukis material in 1978 to the new, prize-winning museum in the Candie Gardens of St. Peter Port has given the visitor and researcher a new focus for the island's archaeology and history.

As in the other islands, public access to the sites is comparatively easy, and most are in adequate condition. In this section, they are arranged by parishes, and few are far from a public road. Bicycles and cars can be hired, and there is an excellent service of buses that run from St. Peter Port around the coast and through the Islands to most parts. As in Jersey, there is no railway.

References are to the Ordnance Survey map of Guernsey at 1:21.120 (3in. to the mile), obtainable in the Island.

PARISH OF CATEL

Câtel Church, statue-menhir (Fig. 14)   WV 30997991

No. 16 or 17 bus to Câtel church. The menhir stands in the churchyard, near the west end of the church.

Discovered in 1878 inside the church, below the chancel floor, this granite menhir measured 1.98m. in length and 0.68m. across the 'shoulders'. It is one of two in Guernsey carved to roughly human shape, the other being La Gran'-Mére du Chimquière (p. 96). At the crown of the head (best seen at the back) and on the back at shoulder level are carved two raised horizontal bands. In front, a U-shaped 'necklace' and two breasts. Chisel-marks at the very top and the removal of one breast suggest deliberate mutilation, while the area enclosed by the necklace is smooth and undamaged. There are no traces of a face.

The necklace and breasts are precisely paralleled in the Seine-Oise-Marne area, where the dominant form of tomb is the gallery-grave—a form absent, on present evidence, in Guernsey, though present in Jersey. The necklace is also reminiscent of the U-shaped carvings in the tombs of Brittany.

Publication: the discovery is described in a note in *Proc. Soc. Antiq. Lond.,* 8, 1879, 32.

PARISH OF FOREST

Le Bourg, Le Perron du Roi   WV 2961 7570

Nos. 10. 11, 12, 13 buses to Forest Stores. The stone is at the west end of the roadside wall on the south side of Forest Road, opposite the Forest Stores. It should be noted, on the right-hand side, by visitors arriving at the airport and travelling into St. Peter Port.

In view of the three cupmarks on the side, and one in front, this stone is clearly of some anqituity, perhaps a menhir or—it has been suggested—part of the lost monument of Le Trépied de Nouettes. It is 1.2m. in height, and has been moved from its original position at the other side of the road. Two large stones in the south-east corner of the church might also be derived from a lost tomb.

The faint inscription, best seen in evening light, dates from no earlier than the 18th century, and reads PERRON DU ROY; the remainder of the inscription is largely illegible. It has been a mounting-block (*perron*) and a boundary-mark of the Royal Fief.

Publication: Numerous publications are summarised in Kendrick (1928), 180.

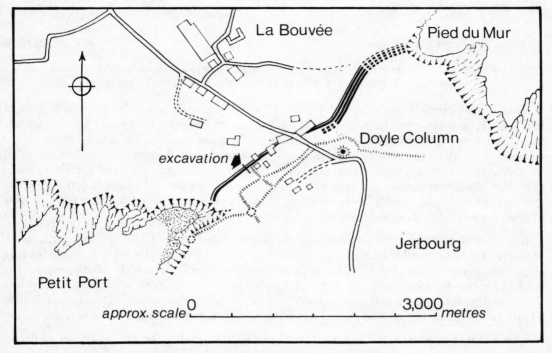

Fig. 49.   Promontory Fort, Jerbourg Point.

Jerbourg, promontory fort

WV 3375

No. 2 bus to Petit Port (Doyle's column)

This was once a multiple defence cutting the promontory of Jerbourg at its narrowest point, where it is only some 3,000m. wide. To the east, a stretch of the triple rampart is still traceable; the western half may have been a single bank and ditch.

That anything of this magnificent earthwork has survived is something of a miracle. The eastern end has been cut by the road and engulfed by the Auberge Divette, whose beer-garden has levelled the northernmost rampart and the intervening ditch. The rampart of the second rises at the southern side of the terrace. West of the road, the rear rampart has made way for a car park, while the small electricity sub-station occupies the central ditch. Conditions improve to the west, with only a series of German bunkers in the ditch and a public lavatory to the south. Finally, the ramparts emerge on the western cliffs with something of their original grandeur, ·overlooking Petit Port to the west and with a steep slope to landward. Further stone-faced earthworks that were once visible to the south of the ramparts and about the foot of the monument have been attributed to a fort of the 14th century A.D., referred to in documents of 1341–7. The current excavations have shown at least three medieval remodellings of the Iron Age rampart (see p. 39), one of which is certainly of this date. A mound near the column, presumably medieval, was removed during the last war. The plan (Fig. 49) is purely provisional, based on the work of

G. T. Derrick and Major Carey Curtis (*Rept. Trans. Soc. Guernesiaise* 4, 1904, 209; 9, 1923, 158–60), with later additions. A definitive plan is in preparation. The current excavations are unpublished.

La Gran'-Mère du Chimquière — WV 32407648

Nos. 2, 4, 7 or 8 bus to The Old Post. The stone stands as the central gatepost at the entrance to the churchyard at the south of the parish church.

This statue-menhir once stood in the churchyard with a cup-marked flat slab at her feet. It is a straight-sided granite slab, 1.67m. in height, cut away to give a square head and sloping shoulders. The solemn face, in good relief with jutting chin, seems to wear a tight head-dress or cap, perhaps decorated with beads, of which a series of four hangs vertically below the neck. Tightly-braided hair apparently falls fanwise over her shoulders above the two carefully-moulded breasts set close together. Below this the arms can be faintly seen, meeting in the centre, and about 0.5m. from the base of the stone is a horizontal band or girdle, also in relief.

She may have originated as a prehistoric statue, like that at Câtel (p. 94), with head, breasts, arms and girdle. However, the evident remodelling of the face, with its lentoid eyes, triangular nose and slit-like mouth, strongly indicate Celtic work; while the formal hair-style might suggest a distant echo of archaic Greek sculpture of the late 6th century B.C. Such influences travelled far in the Celtic world. On these grounds a Gallo-Roman, rather than a Dark Age, date (which has been urged) is preferable.

The crack across the middle of the stone is said to be the result of an abortive attempt (by a churchwarden) to have her removed. Veneration of the statue has certainly continued into historic times; in the 19th century it was considered 'lucky' to place a little offering of fruit or flowers, to spill a few drops of wine at the foot of the statue, or place a coin on her head. As recently as the 1920s she was found decorated with an ivy chaplet on May Day morning, and in 1973 an offering of coins was observed at her feet.

Publication: the best discussion is in Kendrick (1928), 21–5.

PARISH OF ST. PETER IN THE WOOD

La Longue Rocque — WV 26527717

No. 12 or 15 bus to Les Paysans. The menhir stands in a field to the west of Les Paysans, to the south of the house Val des Paysans. It is on private land, and permission should be asked.

This exceptionally long granite shaft stands 3.5m. high, and excavation in 1894 showed a total length of 4.47m. It was embedded in gravel that lay beneath 0.76m. of soil, with a single large trig stone, but no datable finds.

At the foot of this menhir the Guy was formerly burnt on 5 November, a ceremony that is thought in Guernsey to be a continuation of the older practice of burning the effigy of the dying year (le Bout de l'an) at the New Year (de Guérin, 1921, 64).

Publication: J. J. Carey in *Rept. Trans. Guernsey Soc. Nat. Science* 3, 1894, 333.

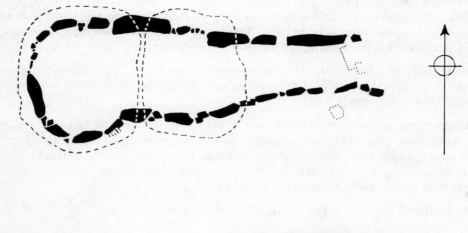

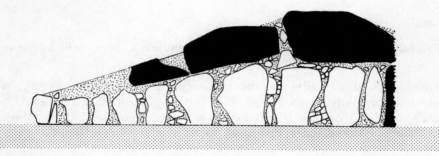

0   5 m

Fig. 50. Le Creux ès Faïes (source: Kendrick 1928).

Le Creux ès Faïes

WV 25077848

Nos. 12, 15, 16, 17 or 33 bus to L'Erée. The tomb entrance faces away from the
angle of the roads that lead to the tip of the promontory. A torch is useful, but
not essential.

This is a well-preserved passage-grave in a low mound, much of which is original
despite wartime disturbance in the south-western portion and the cutting back of
part of the north-east side in 1843 by the then owner of this half. This mutilated face
was subsequently revetted with a wall of re-used material from the peristalith and
mound (or cairn). The first and last of the large stones may be *in situ*; in Lukis's day
the circle was nearly complete, and seven were identified in 1870. Others were
doubtless moved to form a boundary wall across the top of the mound, of which a
few can still be found.

The tomb is of the classic undifferentiated form of the Channel Islands, and the
total length of passage and chamber is 8.5m. It appears (like La Varde, p. 108) to have
been cut into the slope. In the turf at the entrance to the passage lie at least two flat
stones, which may be vestiges of a final blocking. In 1840 Lukis found the chamber

97

filled with recent rubble, and already plundered. There was a hard-trodden floor, 0.45m. thick, of compact earth containing pottery, human and animal bones, and a quantity of burnt vegetable matter. The finds included beakers, a large cinerary urn and a perforated disc of samian, probably a spindle-whorl of Roman date.

Some 6m. to the south-east three stones with a smaller stone at the south-west corner were investigated in 1915. They may be the remains of a small cist, but no datable finds were made.

As its name implies, this tomb was thought to be the abode of fairies; indeed, it was from here that these little people issued on moonlight nights to dance at Mont Saint and on the Catioroc. Drunken soldiers from the nearby barracks used it as a hiding-place—a practice ended by their commanding officer who had it filled with rubble that Lukis had subsequently to remove.

Publication: De Guérin (1915 b); Kendrick (1928), 181–3.

Lihou Island

This little island is privately leased, but open to the public. Access is by a causeway to the mainland at low tide.

Lihou is known principally for the conspicuous remains of a Priory, which has been subjected for many years to sporadic but unpublished excavation. One of the Iron Age cists existed on the Island in Lukis's day (Kendrick, 1928, 186), but has disappeared since. Worked flints, including microliths have been found.

PARISH OF ST. PETER PORT

St. Stephen's Lane   WV 32617851

The stone stands in the front garden of the bungalow Sous L'Eglise in St. Stephen's Lane. It is visible from the road, but is partly obscured by trees.

This possible menhir is of granite, and is about 1.4m. high. It was found recumbent and buried when the bungalow was being built, and was re-erected by the Ancient Monuments Committee. It could be La Petite Longue Rocque recorded in 1793 and 1921 and subsequently lost.

Publication: Cox (1976), 16.

PARISH OF ST. SAMPSON

Route St. Clair   WV 33958121

Nos. 26, 30, 31 or 32 bus to Vale Road. Walk about 50m. up Vale Road to the traffic lights at the junction of Vale Road, Le Murier and St. Clair Hill. The stone is 25m. further on, on the west side of the road in the Fruit Export's Extension Vinery, and is clearly visible from the road.

This squat stone of grey granite is 1.27m. above present ground level, and was discovered in 1960 when a thick hedge was removed. Its depth is considerable, as it proved to be immovably embedded. There are other large half-buried stones nearby and its status as a menhir is uncertain.

Publication: Cox (1976), 21.

Delancey Park
WV 34668105 approx.

> Nos. 30, 31 or 32 bus to Delancey Park. Turn inland and right at the far end of the street to the entrance to the park. The Delancey monument is at the highest point, and the ruined tomb, which has recently been cleared of undergrowth, can be found in the north-east corner of the park, reached by a path behind the tennis courts. The park can also be entered at its northern side.

The large granite slabs of the base of the monument are believed to be re-used from the nearby chambered tomb. This was discovered in 1919 and appeared to be a collapsed parallel-sided passage 9.4m. long and just under 2m. wide, with possible remains of dry-stone walling. No capstones have been positively identified. Scattered stones at the western end may conceivably be from a chamber, but a brief re-examination in 1932 failed to find one, and concluded that it was a gallery-grave.

Finds included part of a probable beaker, burnished but undecorated, coarse undatable sherds, a broken greenstone axe or rubber, and flint waste.

Publication: Rept. Trans. Guernsey Soc. Nat. Sciences 8, 1919, 170 (a brief note on the discovery).

Sandy Hook, L'Islet
WV 33078210

> No. 26 bus to Brookdale. Turn right at L'Islet Methodist church along Sandy Hook Road for 150m., fork left (one-way street), and left again. The site is at the end of this cul-de-sac, on the right behind the council houses.

This remarkable monument was discovered and excavated in 1912, before the surrounding houses were built. It was subsequently neglected and badly vandalised until 1975, when it was tided up by volunteer labour. Sadly, it is deteriorating once more. In view of its unusual nature it urgently needs re-examination and proper protection.

It was found to consist of a roughly D-shaped setting of stones, about 14m. in diameter, with a central cist and 'antechamber'. The cist is 1.72m. in length and 0.76m. wide with a single capstone of triangular section—a feature in which it closely resembles the Tourgis Dolmen in Alderney (p. 129), and to a lesser extent that near Clouet Bay in Sark (p. 121). At each point of the semi-circle was a smaller cist, the northernmost was accompanied by a small stone circle, while the other was enclosed by a slightly larger circle. A pendant circle of stones was found at the south-east corner. A mound is recorded as covering the central cist, which produced a biconical vessel with two pairs of lugs (two perforated, two unperforated). No burials are recorded. The site is oddly low-lying (only 0.3m. above sea level) and material found in the mound (and presumably residual) comprised a tranverse arrowhead of black flint and a class B microlith.

The final form of this monument is hard to interpret from the plan: it is quite clear, though, that it is of more than one phase. The pottery does not help, though that from C might be slightly earlier than that from A. A possible sequence is this:

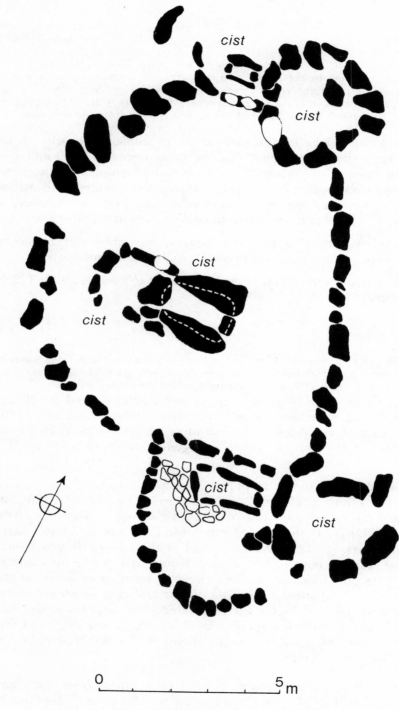

Fig. 51. Sandy Hook, L'Islet (source: Carey Curtis 1912).

the structure was first intended as a simple cist within a circular mound flattened on one side. Subsequently the two 'corners' were cut back and flattened at the sides and secondary cists—each presumably with a mound—were added (the latter apparently still retaining part of its circle). When viewed from the landward side the larger stones of the original peristalith would then have appeared as a straight façade, symmetrically flanked by smaller mounds. This assumes that the central feature *was* a mound and not an open space, as in the Irish 'court cairns'. Finally, perhaps, two smaller mounds with kerbs but no cists were added at the corners. It has been argued above (p. 83) that some passage-graves in the islands were remodelled in more than one phase; this is the only instance in which it can be proposed for an enclosed cist.

A largely unpublished series of photographs is in the Priaulx Library.

Publication: Rept. Trans Guernsey Soc. Nat. Sciences 6, 1912, 401–414.

PARISH OF ST. SAVIOUR

St. Saviour's Church   WV 28077725

> No. 15 bus to St. Saviour's church, or No. 14 to Les Buttes, about 250m. to the
> east of the church. The stone stands at the entrance to the churchyard.

This granite stone is 1.1m. high and bears two deeply incised equal-armed crosses with splayed ends, one on each side. It was originally in the churchyard on the south side of the church, and was moved to its present position when the road wall was built in 1818. The carving on both sides makes the suggestion that it was a consecration stone unlikely; it is even less likely to have been an uninscribed headstone. It must surely be a menhir, christianised by devout parishioners.

Two small cists (both now vanished) were discovered in the churchyard in 1904 and 1908. The first contained a 'few crumbling bones'.

Publication: the three discoveries are summarised by Kendrick (1928), 195.

La Longue Pierre   WV 27107959

> No. 16 or 33 bus to Richmond Stores. Take the road to the tip of the promontory;
> the menir stands on the north side of the (private) drive to Fort Le Crocq.

Incorporated into a field wall, this menhir stands 3m. high. Lukis dug down to its base where he found 'an earthen floor' with pottery and stone rubbers.

There appears to be a second one, 2.1m. high, about 20m. to the west, of red granite. Apart from a possible mention in 1921 it is unrecorded, and was re-erected by the Ancient Monuments Committee in 1955. (*Rept. Trans. Guernsey Soc. Nat. Sciences* 15, 1956, 16.)

Le Trépied, Catioroc   WV 25987889

> Nos. 16, 17 or 33 bus to Perelle Bay. The tomb is in a prominent position on
> raised ground at the southern tip of the bay.

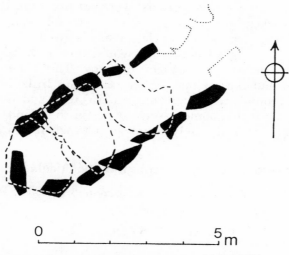

Fig. 52. Le Trépied (source: Kendrick 1928).

This is an almost parallel-sided undifferentiated passage-grave, 5.5m. long, including the scarcely visible stones of a passage of unknown length. There is now no sign of a peristalith, and only a denuded mound. In the chamber there is still over a metre of headroom.

Its reputation for being haunted and the collapse of one capstone had preserved some of its contents when Lukis dug it in 1840. He recovered human bones, parts of at least four beakers, and two barbed and tanged arrowheads. His son restored the collapsed western capstone; this and the westernmost upright collapsed again in 1920 and were re-erected by the States of Guernsey. The internal granite supports represent a third restoration.

This tomb has been a favourite venue for witches, warlocks and fairies, on the evidence of 17th-century witch trials. It is said that the Friday night sabbaths were attended by the Devil himself, in the form of a black goat. Even in the late 19th century it was a dangerous place on a Friday night.

Publication: Kendrick (1928), 188–90.

PARISH OF THE VALE

La Rocque Qui Sonne   WV 34978236

> Nos. 31 or 32 bus to St. Sampson. From the northern corner of the harbour walk
> due north, across the crossroads, for 70m. to the Rue de l'Ecole. The school
> entrance is about 350m. further on, past the right-angled bend in the road.

Standing improbably in the asphalt playground of the Vale schools are two large stones (one, at least, a capstone) and numerous smaller blocks. These are the wreckage of the destruction, in the early 19th century, of a vast passage-grave with a peristalith of which four or five stones are recorded. The diameter of the circle is unknown.

In 1837 Lukis was told a cautionary story which has since been proved to be substantially true. The owner resolved to break it up to build a new house, despite his neighbours' warnings and the eerie ringing sound of the quarryman's hammer which could be heard nearly a mile away. Their predictions were soon fulfilled. For no sooner had the new house been completed than it was burnt to the ground and two of his servants perished in the fire. The remainder of the stone had been broken up as roadmaking material, and the two ships carrying it to England were lost at sea. Fate pursued the man to his next home in Alderney, which in turn was promptly destroyed by fire. Finally, when attempting to return to Guernsey, he himself perished on board in an accident as the ship neared land.

Lukis's subsequent investigations were not complete, and a further examination of the site in 1911 when the schools were built proved inconclusive. However, the known extent of the shattered remains and the sheer quantity of building material derived from the site argue a monument of quite exceptional size, presumably a passage-grave. Finds included beakers (one of them handled), polished axe fragments, a bronze dress-fastener with convex terminals, and a fragment of a decorated jet bracelet.

Publication: Kendrick (1928), 162–165.

Le Déhus   WV 35868303

No. 32 bus to The Dolmen. The monument is (illegibly) signposted from the junction of the main road (Route des Mielles) and Kings Road, and is situated about 100m. along the latter, enclosed by a hedge and a dilapidated wall, adrift in a sea of glasshouses. The gate and door are unlocked, and a torch is essential.

This, one of the finest passage-graves in north-western Europe, has changed its form with successive restorations; for example, two additional side-chambers, both probably spurious, were created as recently as 1933. However, the structure is otherwise essentially as it was when Lukis began excavations in 1837. The mound, about 18m. in diameter, has been convincingly restored to a height of some 3.5m. with a complete peristalith, including dry-stone walling. In plan it is a passage-grave with a short passage 3.35m. long and 0.9m. wide, demarcated by two uprights at its entrance (replaced where Lukis found them). Side-chambers flank the junction of chamber and passage.

The granite pillar supporting the second capstone (counting from the west) is an original feature. On the underside of this capstone is engraved a human figure— principally a face (eyes and mouth, with a natural ridge in the stone for nose) and two hands. Below the hands runs a crescent-shaped design of four grooves, and below this is a circle touching a straight line that runs across the stone. Since the design is partly obscured by the pillar, the slab may have been carved before the erection of the tomb. The main chamber contained vast quantities of limpet shells. The burials here were on two levels, comprising two adults, a child and cremated remains. These were accompanied by a copper tanged dagger and a damaged bell-beaker, of which fragments were also found in the neighbouring side-chamber (A).

103

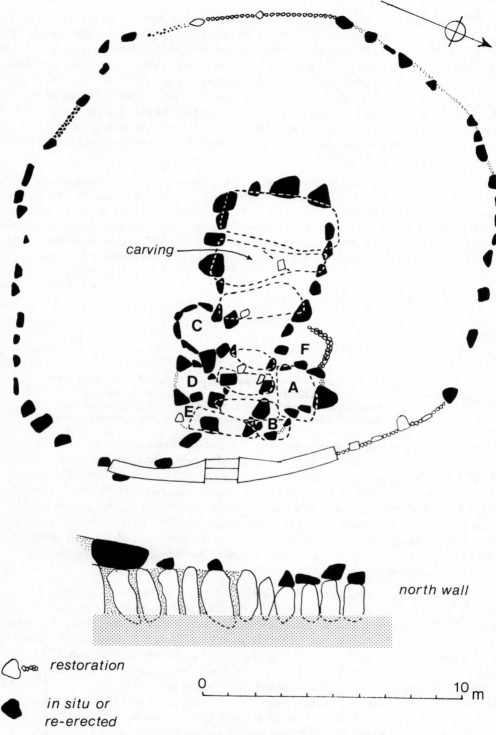

carving

C

F

D

A

E

B

north wall

⬭⟨⟩⟨⟩⟨⟩ restoration

⬛ in situ or
re-erected

0   10 m

Fig. 53.   Le Déhus (source: Collum 1933). (Note slightly reduced scale)

Of the six side-chambers that can be seen today, A–D are authentic. E and F, however, were created in cavities found by the excavators of 1932; these had probably been made by earlier explorers, and were mistaken by the restorers for destroyed side-chambers. Chamber A contained disturbed human remains, several unstratified neolithic and Beaker vessels, and a polished axe of serpentine on a ledge. Chamber B contained the most remarkable burial, whose authenticity we have no reason to doubt—two individuals, side by side, facing in opposite directions, in a kneeling position, upright. Tightly-packed earth and shells kept the remains in position. In chamber C, two layers of filling were separated by a pebble floor. In the lower layer were three bone groups, each with a bowl. In chamber D slab paving separated three levels, of which the two upper layers contained bone heaps, the lowest a pair of undisturbed crouched inhumations with an inverted bowl and a bone point. This is the clearest illustration of the practice of continued use of a tomb by renewing the floor rather than by pushing existing burials aside to make room for the new. Restorations have made this chamber difficult to recognise.

Publication: the earlier work is summarised by Kendrick (1928, 131–158; the carving is discussed by De Guérin (1919) and the 1932 work described by Collum (1933).

L'Ancresse Common

Nos. 30, 31, 32, or 33 bus to L'Ancresse. A few hours' walk westward over the Common and the golf course will take in several sites, and at the end of the walk the No. 30 bus can be taken from Vale church back to St. Peter Port.

Walk about 850m. westwards from the bus terminal along Les Clotures Road to the end of Rocque Balan Lane and a large group of natural rocks will be seen to the north. This is La Rocque Balan, which bears on its flat top two cup-markings, one 22cm. in diameter and 4.5cm. deep, the other 6.3cm. in diameter and 2.5cm. deep.

About 200m. to the north-east of these on No. 16 fairway of the golf course and 30m. from the nearest Martello Tower, is a flat stone partly buried in the turf, with a small cross carved on it. It is 1.5m. long and 0.5m. wide. It was first recorded in 1976 (Cox, 1976, 26–7) and may be a christianised menhir laid low when the golf course was created.

L'Ancresse, unnamed site   WV 30478357

The site is about 90m. south of the Martello Tower that stands in the centre of the sweep of L'Ancresse Bay, on the golf course.

These are the remains of a chamber or cist. Two long stones, 2.1m. long and 0.9m. apart, are probably the sides of a cist, as a third stone is known to have closed the west end. Burials are recorded, but no mound. Six metres to the south-east are five surviving stones of a large circle that in 1837 enclosed two further cists.

Publication: Kendrick (1928), 128–129.

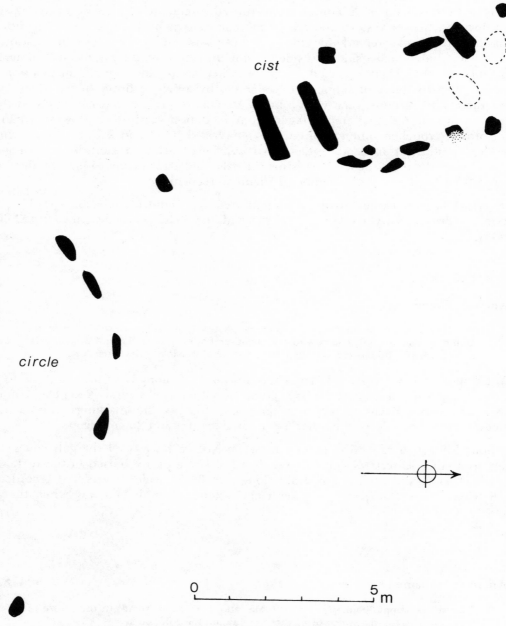

cist

circle

0 — — — — — 5 m

Fig. 54.   L'Ancresse Common, unnamed site (source: Kendrick 1928).

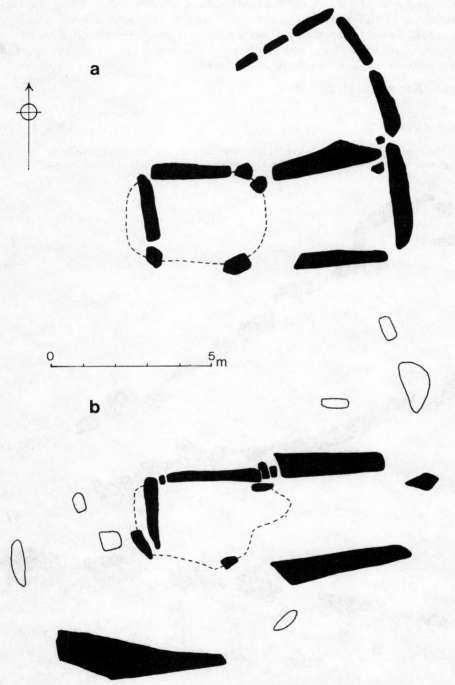

Fig. 55. La Mare ès Mauves a) after Lukis; b) after Kendrick 1928.

L'Ancresse, La Mare ès Mauves   WV 33998354

The site is on the golf course, 100m. west-south-west of the last and to the north-west of a small pond, from which it is named.

These appear to be the ruins of a double cist, 4.5m. by 1.8m. Only the western capstone survives. The closing slab at the east end has disappeared since its discovery in 1837. So, too, has what might have been a second structure attached to the north side. No burials are recorded, but finds included undecorated sherds, perforated stones, stone rubbers and a fragment of a saddle-quern.

Publication: Kendrick (1928), 126–7.

L'Ancresse, La Varde   WV 33698363

Just over 500m. west-north-west of the last is a sandy hillock dominating the golf course and the common. The entrance to the tomb is on the south-east.

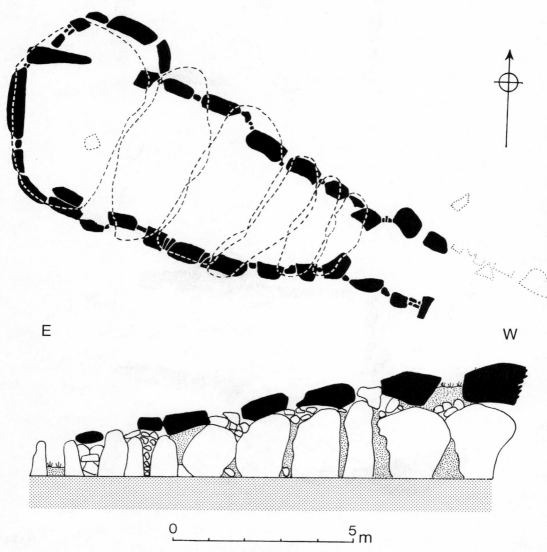

E   W

Fig. 56.   La Varde (source: Kendrick 1928). The section shows the south wall of the tomb.

This impressive passage-grave, 12.5m. long overall, with a chamber 3.6m. wide and 1.8m. high, seems to have been cut into the sandy slope. The peristalith, recorded as almost complete, is now invisible in the gorse, and encloses a mound 18m. in diameter, which has been partly restored. The V-shaped passage of selected slabs graduated in size slopes steadily upwards to the chamber, which is demarcated internally by two narrow uprights. Six out of seven capstones survive, the largest also covering a shallow side-chamber to the north.

The burials were in at least two phases, separated by a layer of limpet shells and pebbles. They comprised over 30 heaps of bones (some of more than one individual, and including at least one child), with some cremated remains in the lower layer. Over 150 urns were identified, all apparently empty. Bones and skull fragments were also found poked between the uprights. The chamber once contained a small slab-lined cist in the floor, which has now disappeared. Finally, the passage was sealed by a dry-stone wall. Finds include decorated and undecorated beakers, a flat serpentine ring, a V-perforated jet button, late Bronze Age urns, Gallo-Roman and samian ware, querns and bronze fragments. Bones included animals, birds and fish. The easternmost capstone in Fig. 56 was illicitly removed before 1870.

Outside, two lines of stones converging on the mound have now disappeared; they may have been field boundaries, as at Les Fouaillages.

Publication: Kendrick (1928), 104–121.

L'Ancresse, La Platte Mare   WV 33578314

Walk 650m. southwards from La Varde, across Mont Cuet Road. The site is on the southern arm of the golf course, by the sixth tee.

This is an irregularly-shaped chamber or cist, with half a capstone in place. An early plan (Fig. 57a) shows that the east side has been altered, making an entrance—perhaps for use as a cattle-pen. On the east end of the north wall are seven cup-markings. A peristalith of 12 stones, but no mound, is recorded, but not now visible (though Kendrick found some of them). Finds included sherds, stone grain-rubbers, and a flint arrowhead.

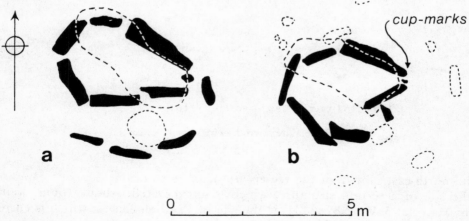

Fig. 57. La Platte Mare: a) in 1842; b) in 1921 (source: Kendrick 1928).

109

Indentations on supporting stone. (idem.)

Fig. 58. La Plate Mare: two drawings by F. C. Lukis.

By the north-east corner of the tee an arc of three stones at the edge of a hollow marks the site of a second structure, which is unexcavated. About 150m. south of La Platte Mare (at WV 33578314) is the site of Les Fouaillages, which is currently under excavation.

Publication: Kendrick (1928), 122–126.

HERM and JETHOU

Herm is in the Bailiwick of Guernsey, and indeed can be clearly seen from St. Peter Port across a channel that is a mere 4–5km. across. The island is 2km. long, from north to south, composed of a particularly fine granite that was not only used in the harbour of St. Peter Port, but exported to London, Manchester, and elsewhere. The heyday of the quarrying, the 1840s, affected all the megalithic structures and saw the total disappearance of several.

As in Guernsey, the high plateau is at the south of the island, yet this half is devoid of megalithic tombs and any traces so far of prehistoric settlement. The northern part is a low-lying sandy plain, bounded by the rising dunes along the north coast; prominent here is the Pierre aux Rats, an obelisk replacing a demolished menhir or dolmen after protests from fishermen who had lost their day-mark. The depth of blown sand in parts of the common can be judged from the position of the megalithic structure at Oyster Point, at the edge of the beach and only 4.5m. above sea-level; borings on the common are reported to have brought up worked flints from a depth of 2–2.5m., though erosion of other parts by wind and human traffic occasionally produces pottery and flint from the prehistoric land surface, possibly indicating settlement here. Moreover, systematic field-walking has produced flint waste from fields at the edge of the plateau. This goes some way to disprove the popular hypothesis, first advanced by Kendrick (1928, 7), that the wealth of prehistoric tombs and the apparent lack of settlement evidence here and in Alderney suggests that they 'were deemed to possess some special virtue as resting-places for the dead—a reputation that may actually have led to the ferrying over of corpses for burial from the much larger island of Guernsey and from the coast of France'. Most of these megalithic structures are grouped on the two prominent rocky eminences of Le Grand Monceau and Le Petit Monceau.

Successive prehistoric periods have left little trace, beyond a fragment of a bronze cauldron (Bronze Age) and some assorted Roman pottery and coins. On the west coast, below Fisherman's Cottage, are exposures of briquetage from salt-working (p. 44); significantly, this briquetage and at least one of the shell-middens in this part of the island were associated with Roman pottery.

The reef of the Pierre Percée rock off the south-west coast is said to be the site of sixth-century chapel to St. Magloire. The early 11th century saw the creation of a Benedictine Abbey on Herm, succeeded by an Augustinian priory in the 12th century and a small Franciscan community in the 15th century. The little chapel of St. Tugual is of unknown date; the first documentary reference to it is of 1480.

Owned and leased by the States of Guernsey, Herm is open to the public and most of the monuments are in the public parts of the island. Much of the land, however, is farmed and permission to enter it should be sought at the harbour. There are facilities for camping, and a large hotel.

Jethou, by contrast, is a private residence and is not open to the public. However, an inspection of the antiquities was allowed in 1975 and the possible megalithic structures are noted below. The only prehistoric object from Jethou now traceable is a circular stone object (Fig. 9c), one of the so-called 'unfinished mace-heads' (see p. 21). It is now in the Guernsey museum. Briquetage has been reported, and at least one shell-midden, of unknown date, can still be found. The island was inhabited by a Benedictine community from 1070 to 1416, and the monks are believed to have created the cultivation terraces in the south and a soil-conservation wall still partly traceable around the coast.

Le Grand Monceau

Although not the highest point in Herm, this steep hill dominates the northern part of the island, rising to 40m. above sea level. From its summit the sites of nearly the extant monuments can be seen. Kendrick's numbering is used in the following descriptions.

About 35m. to the south-east of the summit and on the crest of the hill are the confused remains of a probable megalithic structure (No. 10), whose form could be determined only by excavation. Over a dozen blocks, probably disturbed capstones and uprights, now remain. No finds are known.

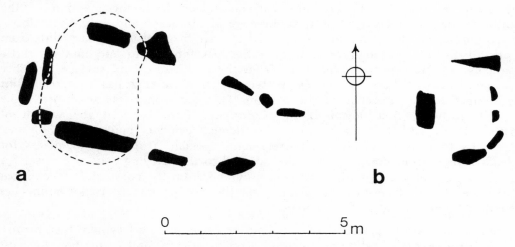

Fig. 59. Two structures in Herm: a) no. 6; b) no. 8 (source: Kendrick 1928).

To the south-west of the summit, and some 9m. below it, a level turf-covered spur runs westwards. On it is a group of three tombs, of which two are identifiable from afar by their growth of brambles. The most easterly (No. 6) was, and probably still is, a well-preserved passage-grave, 6.4m. long with a single collapsed capstone at the west end. This last was supported at both ends when Lukis excavated the site in 1840. He found human bones lying on a bed of pebbles and beneath a layer of limpet shells. 'Ornamented' pottery is recorded.

A second overgrown structure (No. 8) lies 15m. to the north-west of No. 6. This had been used as a quarry before 1844, as was proved by the discovery of a quarryman's iron spike in the excavation. All the stones are now overthrown, but the general shape suggests that this was a cist, not a passage-grave. In Lukis's day there was a flat stone in the centre. Two vessels are recorded—a fragmentary undecorated beaker and a coarse, straight-sided pot, probably of the Bronze Age. Several smaller vessels, now lost, sound like further beakers.

The third structure in this group (No. 9) is about 25m. west-south-west of the last, and is half buried in the turf on the crest of the spur. Five stones form two converging lines 1.5m. apart at the north-western end, 4.5m. apart at the other, 7m. in length overall. Two stones to the north-west, roughly in line with the others, probably continue the structure. A slight hollow suggests that it has been dug into, but no finds are known. The dimensions would be appropriate to a passage-grave.

Le Petit Monceau

Facing Le Grand Monceau on the west is this slightly lower, but equally prominent hill with a summit of exposed rock. The slopes are clothed in bracken intersected by paths; the best approach is by a well-marked path north-westwards from Robert's Cross. Kendrick (1928, 201–4) found most of Lukis's sites with difficulty; by then, quarrying had taken its toll and subsequent depredations (probably during the German Occupation) seem to have removed much of the rest. Kendrick's numbering is retained in the following identifications, which are mostly tentative.

(1) To the east of the path to the summit on a rocky spur to the east-south-east, mostly clear, but with brambles encroaching, this is the most certain identification. Originally it was probably an elongated structure some 4m. long. Before it was first recorded the quarrymen had removed the eastern half of what Lukis's sketch plan suggests was an elongated cist. The chamber, roughly 1.8m. by 1.2m. can still be made out. The uprights were 1.5m. high with dry rubble packing between them.

The peristalith was partly traced, but cannot now be seen. The stratification was more complicated than usual, comprising (from the surface): sand with limpet shells, human and animal bones and much stony rubbish; white sand, more limpet shells and animal bones; yellow earth; a pavement of slabs with human remains; finally more human bones and a great quantity of snail shells (*helix nemoralis*). The burials were thus in two layers, separated by the paving, in distinct heaps. Two pots are recorded— regrettably unstratified—an undecorated beaker, and a straight-sided cup with everted foot, possibly Iron Age.

(2) This is a group of about nine large blocks, apparently a ruined structure with one large stone that has a flattened underside and is probably a displaced capstone. Identification with Kendrick's No. 2 (which was 'close to the preceding structure in an easterly direction') is uncertain. If the identification is correct, this was a cist 2.1m. in length set in an oval enclosure of stones. 'Many skulls' and pottery, decorated and undecorated, were found, including a possible beaker sherd.

An alternative identification is a circular group of stones 19.8m. to the north-east, in which one might possibly see the ruins of a cist with peristalith.

(2a) In open ground but with brambles inside it is a structure that corresponds well to Lukis's sketch plan, but could not be found by Kendrick. It is 8.2m. from No. 1 in an easterly direction. Its contents are unrecorded.

113

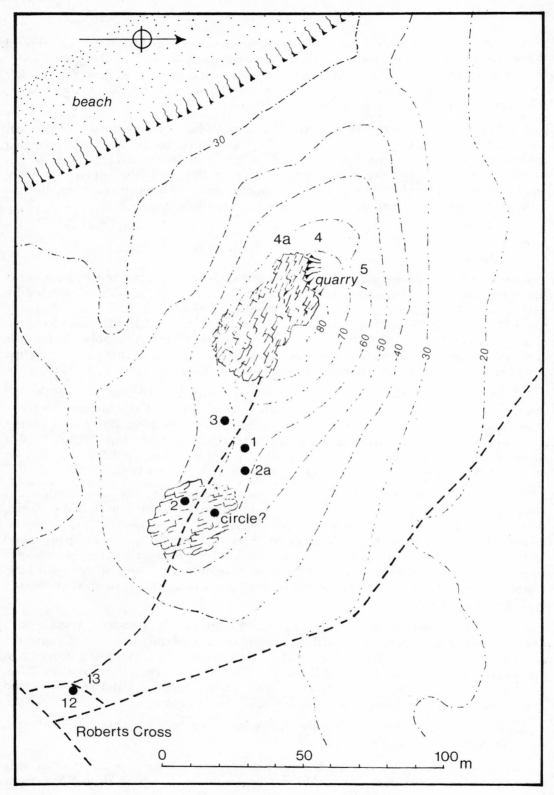

beach

30

4a   4

quarry   5

80
70
60
50
40
30
20

3●

●1

●/2a

2●   ●circle?

●13
12

Roberts Cross

0   50   100 m

Fig. 60.   Herm, Le Petit Monceau. Contours in feet above sea level.

114

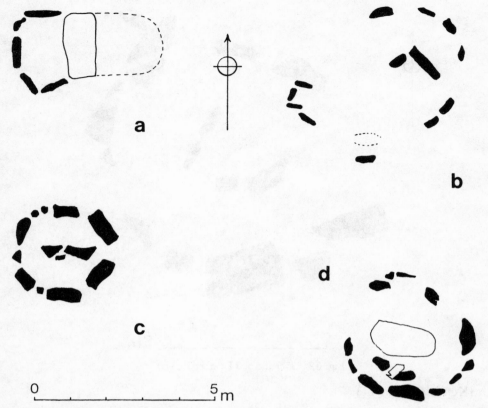

Fig. 61. Structures in Herm: a) No. 1; b) no. 2a; c) no. 3; d) no. 4 (all after Lukis, adjusted).

(3) When studied in 1973 this ruined structure, 10.9m. south-west of No. 1, could not be related to the numbered sites; in 1958, however, it was less overgrown with brambles, and corresponded well with Lukis's sketch plan. About 12 stones can be discerned, forming a rough oval 2.3m. by 2.1m. internally, with a long but broken central slab. Lukis found limpet shells, pebbles, two small sherds and the bones of one person.

(4) The visitor (like the author) may fail to find this one in the luxuriant undergrowth. it was there, however, in 1958, and was found by Dr. Kellett-Smith, who reported 'an ill-defined circle of 16 stones'. F. W. Lukis's sketch plan records 12 in the peristalith, plus 3 others and a capstone. Kendrick confirms that it is 4.2m. across from north to south, and 3.3m. from east to west, the capstones being about 0.9m. in length. It had been cleared before Lukis reached it, and he found only a small sherd without any bones or limpet shells.

(4a) This cist with peristalith, excavated by Lukis, has apparently disappeared. He only implies that it was near No. 4, and says that quarrymen had already broken up the capstone. He found no trace of human remains.

(5) This cist, too, has defied repeated search. We know only that it was on the northern side of the hill, and that in 1842 only one long upright survived; quarrying here continued until at least 1870 (Plate 40), when the trade in Herm granite declined into insignificance.

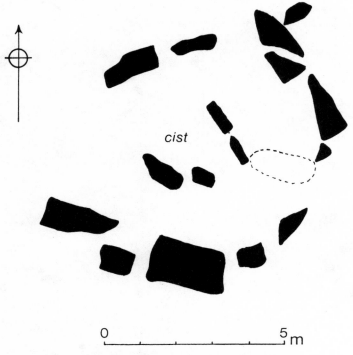

cist

0   5m

Fig. 62.   Herm no. 11 (after Lukis).

Monku (Kendrick, No. 11)

> Monku (formerly Le Monceau) is a hill 48m. above sea-level, overlooking the west
> coast and to the south of the previous sites. The site is in rough ground, on the very
> summit, and is in farmland. Permission to visit it is needed.

Of the cist and enclosing circle recorded by Lukis very little remains today except
the view. When he arrived it was actually being demolished, and in the debris he found
human bones, pottery in large quantities, and masses of limpet shells. None of this
survives. A horseshoe-shaped arrangement of about a dozen very large slabs on edge
was all that survived of a circular, or possibly oval, peristalith; this can still be
recognised in the surviving blocks. The sheer drop to the west is the quarry that
destroyed the monument,

Roberts Cross (Kendrick, No. 12)

> The site is at the intersection of paths in the low ground between Le Grand
> Monceau and Le Petit Monceau, in brambles north-west of the signpost.

The plan of this tomb is unusual. It is a parallel-sided chamber some 4.5m. long
and 2.1m. wide, with a square end to the west and a partition of three low stones
forming an almost square western chamber. Of these last, one survived in 1922, but has
been displaced by 1979. From this point eastwards the walls converge sharply to a very
narrow entrance 0.45m. wide covered by two capstones. Three of the capstones of
the chamber survive. A 0.6m. gap in the middle of the north side might have been an
entrance to the inner chamber; one of two contemporary plans shows it blocked by

116

two low stones. The main entrance, whose parallel jambs form a diminutive passage, was found on excavation in 1841 to have been blocked with dry-stone walling; this was still visible in 1922, but cannot now be seen.

In the chamber the uppermost layer of dark soil contained limpet shells, animal bones and pottery; this rested on a pavement of flat stones, below which a complete skull was found. Below this again was a clay layer with two bell-beakers, one undecorated. To the east of the partition the stratification seems to have been disturbed and to have included a piece of Roman tile. But the clay layer, with human remains sealed by slabs, apparently covered both halves of the chamber.

Interpretation is very difficult. Three outlying upright slabs (none of which can be seen today) suggest a peristalith; this would imply a long mound, 13m. long, with the chamber(s) towards one end. However, even allowing for the partition and a possible side-entrance, this is by no means an orthodox gallery-grave. Nor is it a typical passage-grave, though it is tempting to see the nearest outlying upright as part of a side-chamber entered from the gap in the north wall. This stone is 1.8m. away, and Lukis, who cut a trench to it, found no sign of a chamber.

There was once a second structure (Kendrick, No. 13) about 8.2m. north-west of the western capstone of the last, which cannot now be indentified in the undergrowth. It seems to have been an interesting structure; although Lukis's plans are contradictory and confusing, it may represent the chamber of a passage-grave attached to an earlier ruined structure. Kendrick's suggestion (1928, 211) that 'the chamber must have been erected on a site already partly occupied by a small cist-burial' reverses the

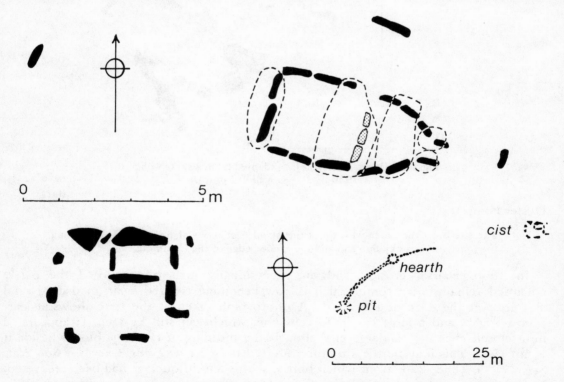

Fig. 63. Herm: a) no. 12 (Roberts Cross), from Lukis, with additions in 1922 (source: Kendrick 1928); b), c), no. 15, plan and associated structures (after Lukis).

117

accepted sequence of these tombs. It does seem, however, that this was a structure of more than one phase whose sequence may never be elucidated. The finds included a wide variety of shells, human remains, an early round-bottomed pot with some beakers and a piece of a shale ornament.

The Common

The site is in a hollow, the lowest point on the Common, in the centre just to the east of a direct line between the obelisk and the summit of Le Grand Monceau.

There is a slab-lined cist (Kendrick, No. 15), 1.3m. by 1.06m., visible about 0.7m. deep in the north-east quadrant of a stone circle, presumably the peristalith of a mound about 3m. in diameter. This cist contained 'shells, mullers and pottery', and to the west of the cist was a 'large vase with handles and markings' (now lost); no trace was found of human remains.

Associated with the cist is a curved line of stones, incorporating a stone-lined hearth and ending in a pit, that once led away to the south-west. The line becomes a double line beyond the hearth, and is presumably the base of an ancient wall. These features were traceable as recently as 1970, but they are now practically covered by the turf.

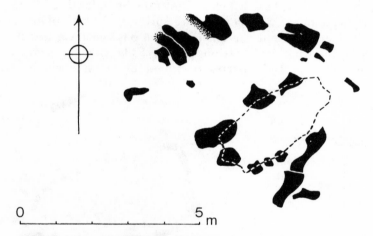

Fig. 64.   Herm, Oyster Point (adapted from a sketch-plan of
1950 by Dr. R. Kellett-Smith).

Oyster Point

The site is on the north-west tip of the island, just above high-tide mark, between a
rocky outcrop and the eroded edge of the Common.

In 1950, coastal erosion and an exceptionally high tide exposed the partly collapsed remains of a tomb which is now becoming covered again in drifted sand and grass at the edge of the dunes. A photograph taken at the time shows at least four uprights and a large displaced capstone, which can still be seen. It appears to be a closed chamber, or large cist, though the meaning of the large blocks beside it is not clear. This may be the structure referred to in *Rept. Trans. Guernsey Soc. Nat. Sciences*, 5, 1898, 260, from which bones, sherds and briquetage had been recovered. No excavation is known. The plan (fig. 64) is adapted from a sketch plan of 1950. The surrounding stones were regarded at the time as a very doubtful peristalith.

Jethou

Numerous 'cromlechs', a 'stone circle' and a 'line of stones' have been identified in the past and claimed as prehistoric (Cliff, 1960, *passim*). Of the alleged circle, only 3–4 stones are now visible, and they are not an arc of a circle. The line of stones (south-west of the Gibbet) is more probably the ruins of a field or boundary wall, continuing the line of an existing wall to the north.

At least two shell-middens with briquetage have been noted in the past, and one (without briquetage) was noted in 1975 to the west of the house.

A small slab-lined pit near the Gibbet site, on the highest point of the island, is now very overgrown. It is certainly artificial, and may conceivably be a megalithic cist without a capstone.

There are three supposed menhirs on the island. One (on the east coast) could not be identified in 1975; the other two look genuine.

(a) In Cannon Field, in the centre of the island, is a stone about 1.14m. high, roughly wedge-shaped and pointed, and with no surface markings. Flint implements (not now traceable) were said to have been found under it in 1959.

(b) In Fairy Wood, at the north end of the avenue, is a pointed stone, 1.06m. high, unworked except for a hole bored from the south side, perhaps for use as a gate-post. The claim that this stone, the obelisk on Herm and the Pierre Percée are in line is incorrect; even had the hole completely pierced the standing stone it would not have pointed towards either of the other supposed markers.

As stated above, Jethou is now inaccessible to visitors. One feature, however, can be seen from the ferry-boats between Herm and Guernsey as they pass the southern tip of the island. This is Les Côtes, a series of cultivation terraces on the south-facing slope which are attributed to the Benedictine community in residence from 1070 to 1416.

Publication: Kendrick (1928), 221–2; Cliff (1960).

119

SARK

Sark lies 12km. to the east of Guernsey, and is in the Guernsey Bailiwick. It is virtually two islands, Great and Little Sark, each a plateau with precipitous rocky cliffs, joined by the famous narrow isthmus known as La Coupée. Granite is found at both ends of the island, and small amounts of tin, lead and silver have been mined in Little Sark. The remains of the silver mines recall an interesting story of determination and financial disaster outside the scope of this book, but well told by Ewen and de Carteret (1969, 98–102); visitors should be strongly warned that the exploration of the abandoned workings is extremely dangerous. It should be noted, however, that there is no evidence that these deposits were exploited in the prehistoric or Roman periods. The cliffs of Sark contain several caves, one or two of which might have been suitable for Palaeolithic occupation. No traces have been recorded so far.

Few prehistoric monuments survive today. Writing in 1874, the Rev. J. L. V. Cachemaille observed (1928, 8–9), 'Small as it is, Sark possessed several cromlechs, some of which were large; others of moderate size; others again are simply cysts. Not many years since, the whereabouts of ten cromlechs could be perfectly distinguished; but all have now disappeared, with the exception of two nearly entire cysts. A few great stones which originally belonged to these cromlechs may still be seen here and there, the rest have been broken up to construct walls and houses'. The two cists recently recognised as authentic (pp. 121-4) are presumably those referred to; they are, however, on private land and can be visited only by special arrangement. For the rest, the visitor can but speculate about the source of the very large stones used in the field-walls of the island (Plate 25), often as gate-posts; one in particular (Plate 20), about 120m. south of La Vaurocque crossroads, has the shouldered form of a possible statue-menhir (for these, see p. 30). Cachemaille mentions many 'stone troughs and mullers' and 'quantities of stone knives, hammers, amulets or discs of stone and clay-beads' and 'fragments of Celtic pottery made by hand'. Several polished neolithic axes are still extant, in the Guernsey museum and in private hands, and Bronze Age occupation is attested by a flat copper axe and the tip of another. These may be the survivors of a founder's hoard, as they are reported (Kendrick, 1928, 222) to have been associated with numerous other bronzes and several 'anvil-stones'.

Cachemaille's 'discs of stone' are probably the 'rouettes de faïtiaux' or fairy rings shown in Fig. 20. They are made of various stones, including beach-pebble, and (in spite of their apparent lack of balance) are probably spindle-whorls.

They are a Sark speciality, and comparison of the incised radial lines with a pottery whorl from Les Huguettes, Alderney, suggests a late Bronze Age or early Iron Age date for the settlement they represent. The full Iron Age is represented by the famous

'Sark Hoard' (p. 42 and Plate 35). Cachemaille also records a particularly mysterious item that may belong to this period: 'numbers of earthy holes, two or three feet deep, containing pottery and cinders . . . found close together in certain localities', which he interpreted as cooking-pits. These have not been seen since. Fieldwork has, moreover, failed to find any signs of briquetage from salt-boiling, or shell-middens. A possible promontory earthwork cutting the headland of L'Eperquerie (p. 125) may be of Iron Age date; so, too, may a crudely-carved and possibly 'Celtic' head photographed in 1965 and now lost (*Guernsey Weekly Press*, 6 July 1965).

For the Roman period we have merely vague references to coins and samian pottery, a drawing of a quern in the Lukis papers, and an unverifiable tradition of a Roman mining interest in Little Sark (p. 126). The first appearance of Sark in the written record is a legendary account (probably of the 10th century) of the landing of St. Magloire in A.D. 565 (Ewen and de Carteret, 1969, 16-17).

The only archaeological excavation in the Island took place in 1980, but regular fieldwork and research is now carried out by members of the newly-formed Société Sercquiaise. There is no museum in the Island.

Sark is reached either by the regular boats from St. Peter Port, or by the less frequent hydrofoil from Alderney and Guernsey. Most parts of the Island are accessible to visitors by public roads and paths, but permission should always be asked before entering farmland. There are no cars on Sark, but bicycles can be hired. The official maps are at the scale of 1:10,560, or 6in. to the mile.

La Vaurocque   WV 46147574

Six slabs line the road at the south-east corner of La Vaurocque crossroads, with
a further upright in the wall opposite.

These seven blocks are believed to be from a demolished megalithic structure, of which nothing else is known. 'Several relics of clay and stone have been found near the place', wrote Lukis, 'as well as a perfect celt of tremolite'.

A nearby courtil was the find-spot in 1718 of the 'Sark Hoard' (p. 42), and about 180m. to the north-east is the only known flint-working site in the island.

Clouet Bay   WV 45567350

The site is in an inaccessible position on the southern cliffs of Little Sark, in thick
gorse and brambles. It is strictly private, and intending visitors are asked to contact
the caretaker at the Barracks (Tel.: 2192) in advance.

This partly ruined cist was excavated by the Société Sercquiaise in 1980 and was found to have been disturbed in two places. Nearly all the stones are displaced by cliffside erosion and later disturbance, even possibly by one of the earthquakes to which the Channel Islands were subject during the Middle Ages (Mourant, 1931, 1936). It is crudely constructed of diorite blocks of various shapes and sizes, all of which could have been obtained from the site itself or nearby, needing only to be moved sideways or downwards. Quarrying might have emphasised the roughly rectangular niche or platform on which the structure stands. The bedrock is a soft, decayed granite with outcrops of hard quartz diorite; one such outcrop provided a secure base to the

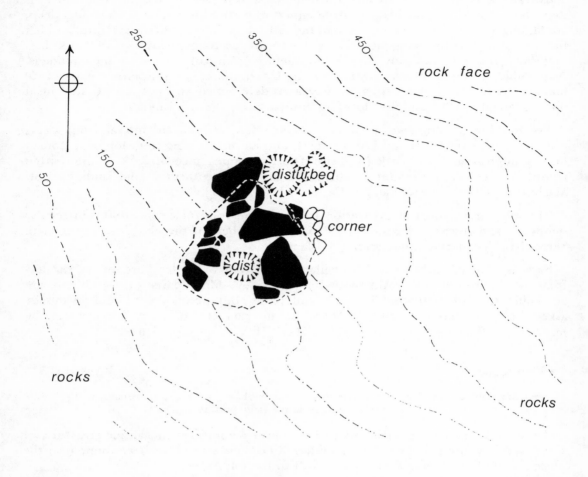

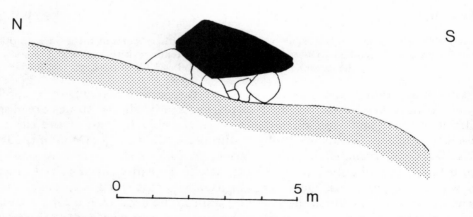

Fig. 65. Clouet Bay, Sark. Contours in centimetres above arbitrary bench-mark.

south and west, below which the ground falls away at a 45deg. angle. A level floor for the cist was cut into the soft granite bedrock; one stone-lined corner of this was identified in the excavation. Possible axe-polishing grooves can be seen on the eastern side of the capstone, presumably made before it was moved into position. Slight traces of the rubble mound or cairn were identified on the eastern side; it is possible that the more portable material of this may have been plundered for building nearby field-walls, leaving erosion to remove the rest. One or more uprights are missing on the downhill side. In view of the shape of the site the whole may have been D-shaped. The interior has been scoured by erosion and damaged by recent digging. No trace of a grave survived.

The triangular section of the capstone resembles those of the smaller cists at Sandy Hook, Guernsey (p. 99) and Tourgis, Alderney (p. 129). Its cliffside situation is unusual, shared only by the other survivor in Sark, La Vermandaye and possibly also by La Roche à la Fée, Jersey (p. 91). In both the crudity of construction and economy of effort suggest that they are late in the series of megalithic structures in the Channel Islands.

A concentration of flints above the site, to the south and west of the barracks, suggests a possible settlement site. A single prehistoric sherd and a large dolerite axe or hammer support this suggestion.

Publication: a full report on the excavation is in preparation (Johnston, forthcoming).

La Vermandaye   WV 45457249

This site is on private land and not accessible to the public. Permission to visit should be asked at Duval Farm. From the farm follow the field-boundaries to the west and north of the ruined windmill. Beyond the cultivated area the cliffs suddenly fall away to a rocky inlet; a hollow track, visible only when the bracken is low, leads down the cliff past the site. The cist stands half-way down the steep slope below a prominent outcrop of rock, and is invisible from above.

It is probably that mentioned by Kendrick (1928, 223). He did not visit it, and was told that it is probably a natural formation. It appears, however, to be a small cist, with the closing slab on the downhill side missing; this, perhaps, is the stone lying buried in front. No burials or finds are known.

It does, however, share many features with the excavated example at Clouet Bay. Both are roughly constructed rectangles, each with a triangular capstone. In each case the stones could be easily found nearby and moved downhill. The rear wall of the chamber at Vermandaye is a vertical rock surface, though only excavation could show whether this is the result of quarrying or the deliberate choice of a natural feature; in either case, it resembles the excavated cavity at Clouet Bay. The most striking similarity, however, is the choice of a cliffside setting, below the crest and overlooking the sea—a rare situation for a cist in the Channel Islands. Insular peculiarities can be detected in the passage-graves of the Islands; and in these two cists we may be seeing a choice of site peculiar to this Island.

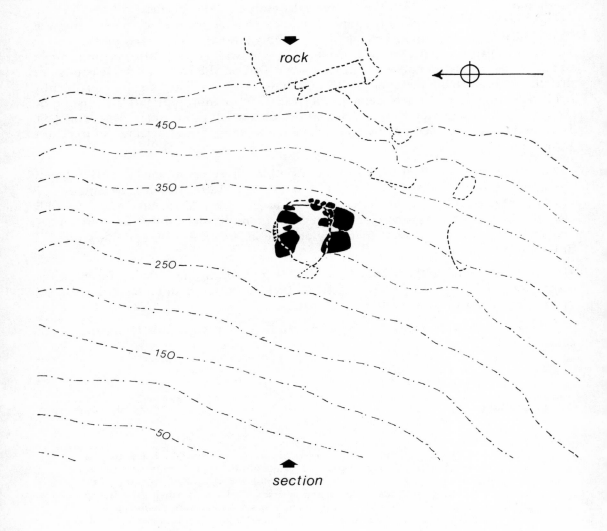

rock

section

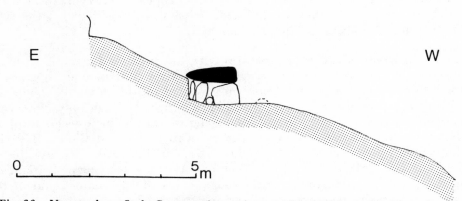

E   W

0   5 m

Fig. 66.   Vermandaye, Sark. Contours in centimetres above arbitrary bench-mark.

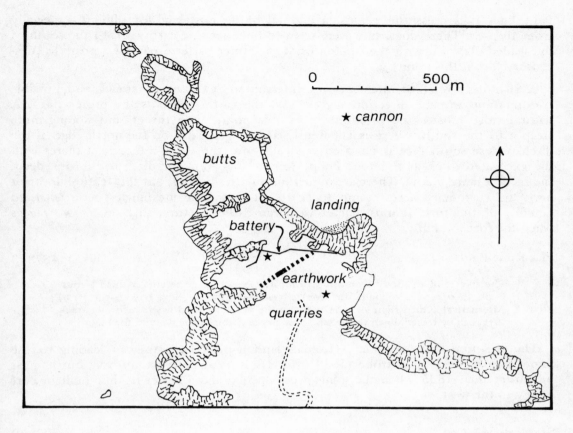

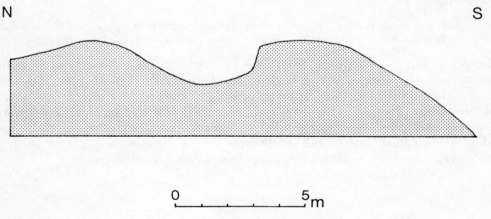

Fig. 67. L'Eperquerie, Sark.

L'Eperquerie

WV 46157761

The Rue de la Moinerie leads northwards to Eperquerie Common. Take the
footpath continuing the line of the road.

The northern tip of Sark is traditionally believed to have been cut off by two
earthworks of unknown date. One or both of these might be explained by the two

fault lines that cross the peninsula and might be mistaken for ditches, especially from the sea. There does, however, seem to be a genuine earthwork to the south of the walled platform with the cannon on it (a former battery, part of a possible 16th-century fort at this point).

A 20–30m. stretch of ditch survives, interrupted by causeways at each end; possible continuations in each direction suggest that the earthwork cuts the promontory. A natural ridge crosses the promontory at this point, with the ground sloping more steeply to the south. There is apparently a denuded bank on the north edge of the ditch, whose south face is quarried vertically into the rock—a feature it shares with the excavated ditch at Frémont Point, Jersey (Fig. 40). The ditch is *c.*1.75m. deep, the bank a mere 0.25m. There are numerous quarries nearby, but this feature does not have the customary access ramp for carts. It would be meaningless as a rearward defence of the fort. It must therefore be an earlier feature, slighted in two places when the fort was built.

Plat Roue Bay   WV 45467328

> The bay is in the southernmost tip of Little Sark. Take the cliff path to Venus'
> Pool, then scramble round the rocky headland into the next bay to the West.
> Alternatively, turn right off the path on the bare headland where a former track
> can be traced down to the bay. Masonry is visible at the head of the bay.

The tradition that this was a Roman landing-place or causeway leading to the mines is preserved by Latrobe (1914, 45). Its Roman date is unproven, but it must be earlier than 1835 when the mines were opened and a better landing built in Port Gorey to the west.

St. Magloire's Cell   WV 46307652

> The site is the private gardens of the Seigneurie, open to the public on Mondays.
> It is an inconspicuous group of stones by the triple arched opening in the wall.

In A.D. 565 St. Magloire, from Dol in Brittany, built his cell and founded a monastery for 62 monks. Viking raids drove the monks out in 840, but they returned and remained until 1463. The supposed remains of the cell are protected by a tradition that prophesies doom to anyone who moves them. Of the medieval monastery two (of three) carp ponds and masonry of a water-mill survive to the south of the land leading to *L'Ecluse* hotel, and north-west to the Seigneurie. The other monastic remains—an impressive wall and two chapels—are certainly medieval.

ALDERNEY

Alderney is the nearest of the Channel Islands to France, and the most northerly. In antiquity, access by sea from the mainland would have been difficult; for the north-east corner, only 14.5km. from the mainland, is cut off from it by The Race, where fierce tides run at up to seven knots, while off the west and south-west corner The Swinge runs almost as fast amid a complex of submerged reefs. The long south-east side of the island is crowned by rugged cliffs and offers one refuge only, Longis Bay. This was a harbour from Roman times until at least the later Middle Ages.

The island is 7km. long and 2km. at its widest, composed in its western half of granodiorite, the eastern half being divided roughly longitudinally between the diorite of the northern side and the Alderney sandstone to the south and east. There is a limited amount of gabbro and granite. While the town of St. Anne's and the well-preserved traces of its medieval open fields occupy the plateau of the south-western half, prehistoric and Roman settlers seem to have preferred the Longis end of the island. One site is marked by a shell midden and worked flints beyond the old rifle range at the eastern end of the sea wall; on Longis Common was found one of the finest Bronze Age hoards in the Islands; the Iron Age structure at Les Huguettes was the focus of a settlement of unknown extent at the edge of the Common, perhaps overlooked by a promontory fort on Essex Hill; and excavations by The Nunnery, a small fort of supposed Roman origins, have given glimpses of a Gallo-Roman settlement with masonry buildings. Alternative neolithic settlement at the extreme south-west end of the island is suggested by the tombs and the discovery of a flint-working site beneath the Tourgis Dolmen. This possible polarisation of settlement is reflected in the concentration of tombs and cemeteries at the extreme ends of the island.

Time has dealt more harshly with the monuments of Alderney than elsewhere in the Channel Islands. The density of fortifications from medival times to the Napoleonic era and the Second World War have made it one of the most heavily fortified parts of Europe; to the fort-builders of the 19th century and the German occupation of the 20th century we owe the destruction, with but scanty record, of most of the monuments. Of the seven survivors described here, only three merit prolonged study. However, the efforts of the Alderney Society, and in particular their museum in St. Anne's, more than compensate for the loss.

The visitor will find that all parts of the island are within easy walking distance of St. Anne or anywhere else, and that it is not feasible to bring a car. Numerous cars have indeed reached the island somehow, and a few are for hire—as are bicycles. A bus circles the island regularly, frequently in the holiday season. There are footpaths in plenty, and public access to the sites is easy, except where indicated.

References are to the 1:10,560 (i.e., 6in. to mile) map of Alderney. It is usually available in the island, but it is safer to obtain one in advance of a visit.

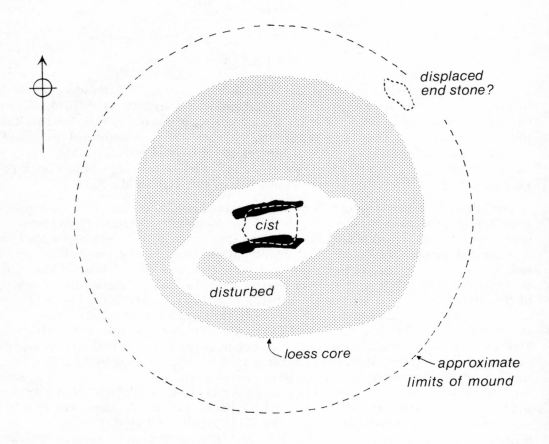

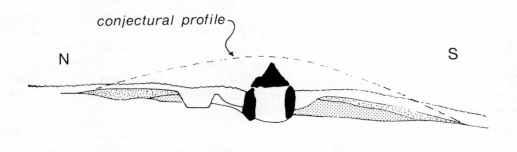

Fig. 68. The Tourgis Dolmen, Alderney (source: Johnston 1974).

The Tourgis Dolmen (Roc à l'Epine)

The site is west of the road running south from Fort Tourgis towards the airport,
some 200m. of the fort. It is in a clearing in the gorse, visible from the road.

This attractive little cist has been dug into twice at least. It was re-discovered after
the war by the Alderney Society and totally excavated by them in 1974. This was
followed by consolidation and partial restoration of the structure by the Society, who
rent the site from the States of Alderney and maintain it scrupulously.

The mound is less than a metre in height, and was found on excavation to be a
circle of about 12.8m.: the core was of the local loess, originally capped by purplish-
brown sandy soil with granite fragments and flint waste scraped up from the
surrounding surface. The central area was severely disturbed. There was no sign of
a kerb, and an isolated block found at the north-eastern edge of the mound has been
restored to its probable position closing one end of the cist.

The cist itself measured a mere 2m. by 0.8m. internally, being built of large slabs
of the western grandodiorite with a single capstone. The triangular section of the
latter resembles that of the central cist at Sandy Hook, Guernsey (p. 99). We do
not know if it was correctly replaced in 1830; it was temporarily removed during the
1974 excavation. Apart from one flake, the cist was devoid of finds in 1974, but
'urns and other articles' were found before 1838, and a 'flint knife' in 1853. A tiny
sherd (apparently prehistoric) was found on the surface near the cist in 1970.

An important discovery under the mound was a flint-working area with tools,
flint waste, and half-finished artifacts. This has helped our understanding of the
problems of working the poor flint available in the islands.

The Tourgis Dolmen was originally part of a group including at least two or three
others, now destroyed. A further group, including the lost Houguette de la Taillie,
also once existed in the south-west corner of the island.

Publication: Johnston (1976).

Les Rochers

A track leads east from Valongis towards the radio masts. Skirt the perimeter of the
radio station to the south and east. The site is in a clearing in the brambles about
70m. east of the masts.

In 1838 a small mound was investigated on Les Rochers, the highest part of the
island. In recent years the Alderney Society has found and cleared what might be its
denunded remains.

In the original discovery, two stone slabs leaning against one another covered some
animal bones, while a small cist containing two sherds was found nearby. Today, 10
large blocks, one of which might have been a capstone, form an elongated group 8m.
long. An arc of small blocks to the north may represent a peristalith, perhaps 15–20m.
in diameter.

The site is confused by the loose boulders hereabouts, of natural origin, after which
the place is named. In the absence of fresh excavation, this group of stones must be
regarded as a very doubtful megalith.

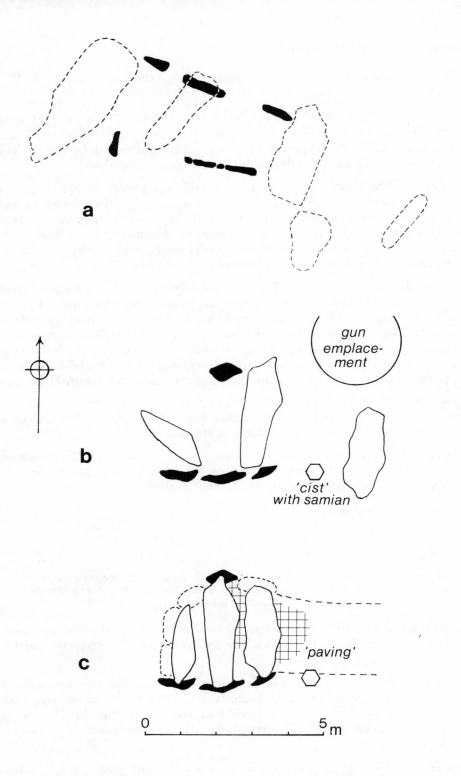

a

b

gun emplace-ment

'cist' with samian

c

'paving'

0   5 m

Fig. 69. Alderney: a) Les Pourciaux North, as in 1921 (source: Kendrick
1928); b) Les Pourciaux South, as in 1921 (Kendrick) with cist (Lukis) and
wartime gun emplacement; c) suggested restoration (source: Johnston 1973).

The sites are on the southern brow of the plateau at the north-east end of the
Island, overlooking Longis Common. They are on private land and anyone wishing
to visit them should write first to the museum, who may be able to arrange access.

Les Pourciaux North is now so badly damaged by its war-time conversion into a
gun-emplacement that re-examination seems impossible. Lukis's plan of 1853 suggests
that it was a gallery-grave at least 8m. long with parallel sides 1.5m. apart; three
capstones are shown in place, with a fourth lying by the dry-stone wall that closed
the south-east end. No entrances can be detected; there are two gaps in the orthostats,
at the southern corner and in the mid-point of the north-eastern side, while the
north-western corner has been disturbed. The north-western end was apparently not
closed. Kendrick's plan of 1921, however, suggests a wedge-shaped structure, a form
confirmed by the wreckage in its present state.

Lukis's section records three strata, the uppermost being blown sand, the middle
one containing animal bones, and the lowest of black soil with human bones and
limpet shells, on a paved floor. Several small internal cists once existed, of which
we have a record of one in the south-east corner (no finds reported) and a cluster of
rectangular miniature cells against the western wall (Plate 11); each was covered by
a small slab, and each contained a skull and other human remains, but no pottery.
The only pottery that survives from this monument is two Roman vessels, their
relatively complete state suggesting a funerary re-use of the tomb, from the settlement
on the Common below. The only other finds seem to have been a possible anvil-stone
and a polished stone axe. The most acceptable interpretation of this curious site is
that it was an undifferentiated passage-grave with its north-western end lost and its
south-western end blocked by dry-stone walling. The final prehistoric insertion may
have been the single cist at this end. If the tomb was used to capacity and sealed, its
successor would be the smaller passage-grave to the south of it.

Les Pourciaux South is now merely a heap of small stones and a depression, the
result of an excavation by the Alderney Society in 1973 that attempted to re-discover
the site after its war-time disappearance.

The only clues to its location were the distance of 62ft. (18.8m.) between the two
structures, recorded by Lukis, a photograph of about 1906 and Kendrick's photograph
(1921, Pl. XIX). These show the substantial remains of a ruined passage-grave, which
the excavators concluded was entirely removed by the German gunners in the creation
of a circular, concrete gun-emplacement; apparently it had already been partly
demolished in antiquity.

Enough information, however, has survived to enable a reconstruction to be made
on paper. It is of small passage-grave with a chamber about 4.5m. long by 3m. at its
widest, three or more capstones, and a paved floor. There were at least three or four
vessels in the chamber (all of them now lost), one at least of which was probably a
very late piece. Partial demolition in antiquity had removed the entire passage, and
a samian sherd in what might be the packing of one upright. Lukis's 'cist with samian'
suggests a possibly Roman date for this first desecration of the tomb. Lukis also
recorded 'paving and pottery'.

Publication: the northern monument is discussed in detail by Kendrick (1921),
229–32; the other by Johnston (1973).

Note.—The 'insignificant ruins' of a cist some 27m. to the south-west of the southern monument were recorded by Lukis and survived until Kendrick's day; this site, too, must have perished during the Occupation.

Les Huguettes

From the Nunnery, take the road northwards towards the Coastguards' Cottages. After about 800m. a path to the left leads towards the lower end of the golf course and the site.

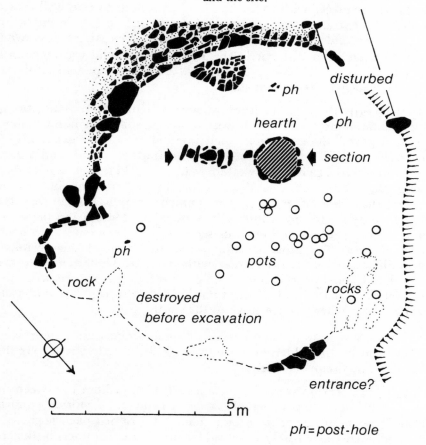

ph = post-hole

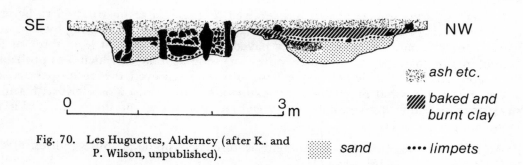

ash etc.

baked and burnt clay

sand

limpets

Fig. 70. Les Huguettes, Alderney (after K. and P. Wilson, unpublished).

Since its accidental discovery and subsequent excavation by the Alderney Society between 1968 and 1970, the site has been meticulously restored and is maintained by the Society.

A circular dry-stone wall about 9m. in diameter, enclosed a central circular hearth and a semi-circular stone platform to the south. This last adjoined the wall, but was separated from it by a narrow channel. Near it were thick deposits of ash, with considerable quantities of pottery and animal bones. A radio-carbon date (uncalibrated) for the deposit was 490 B.C.$\pm$ 100. Finds included a late Bronze Age bifid razor, clay loomweights, bronze tweezers, a bone 'weaving-comb', a stone with three perforations (perhaps for rope-making), and stone tools, probably for smoothing pots. A total of 70 identifiable pots was found; of these, the complete section of 22 can be drawn (these are on show in the museum), and the almost complete section of 37 more. Petrological examination at Southampton has confirmed that all or most are of local manufacture.

This evidence suggests a communal domestic late Bronze Age or early Iron Age site with pottery-making and -firing in a large bonfire: a discovery believed to be unique. It was the focus of a community of unknown extent, since at least one hut-site can be seen nearby. The pottery shows that this is contemporary with the enigmatic stone structure partly excavated at The Kennels nearby (p. 38). The excavation report is in preparation.

Essex Hill

An attractive walk leads up a metalled road from The Longis Road to Essex Castle and by a lane westwards over the summit to rejoin the road near the golf course. The fields to the north are private, the clifftop paths are common land.

In 1847 an earthwork here was described as 'a sort of entrenchment or dyke, running from the southern cliffs northwards'. Essex Hill is the most likely site for a promontory fort in Alderney, but the site of this earthwork is now lost amid the disturbance caused by the old telegraph station, German bunkers, cultivation and undergrowth. However, it is sometimes possible, in evening sunlight, to detect what may be a faint denuded rampart (rather than a lynchet) at the edge of the field immediately north-west of Essex Castle, on the very crest. This loses itself in the bracken to the west; beyond this the field has been so scoured by cultivation that, if any landward defences ever existed, no trace survives. Oyster shells and many worked flints have been found on the surface. It is possible that a short stretch of double lynchet at WA 5915 0780 preserves the line, overlooking the deep valley along which the Longis Road runs.

Publication: the initial reference is in *Journ. Brit. Archaeol. Assoc.* 3, 1847, 6.

The Nunnery (Les Murs de Bas, Le Fort des Murs)   WA 59510813

The fort stands at the western side of Longis Bay. It is privately leased from the States of Alderney, and the interior is not accessible to visitors.

This little fort is traditionally a Roman building, much modified; an analysis of its present state suggests four broad phases, into which complex alterations must be fitted. A conjectural phase I comprises a rectangular curtain wall with rounded

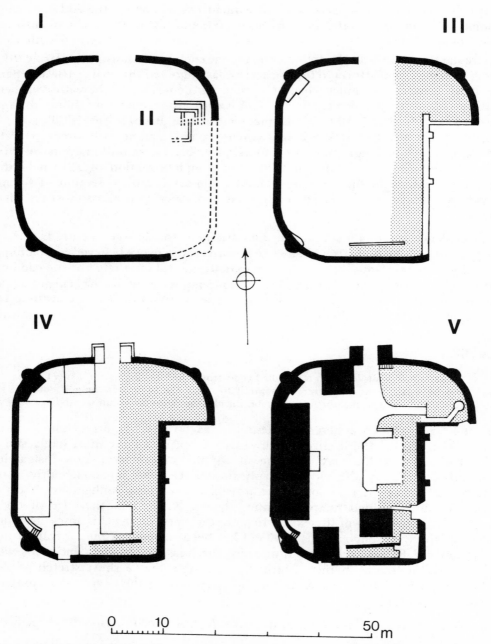

Fig. 71. The Nunnery, Alderney (from a new survey by A. Johnston). Provisional phases.

corners and shallow corner-bastions and a single entrance of unknown form. This is all that one can claim (with serious reservations) to be Roman. Two sets of fragmentary foundations are provisionally assigned to phase II, that to the south can still be traced, but the rest (recorded by Kendrick, 1921, Fig. 126) were destroyed in the War. At some stage, coastal erosion caused part of the curtain and one bastion to collapse on to the beach, and in phase III a new buttressed wall was

134

constructed to retain a massive bank and a walled ramp—evidently to mount cannon. Our earliest documentary reference is to a 'blockhouse' built below Essex Castle in about 1435, and in 1540 the fort of 'Lunges' was supplied with cannon from Castle Cornet in Guernsey. In 1584 it was converted to a private house; by 1735 it was 'utterly ruined' and a plan of that date shows an unintelligible complex of internal buildings. In 1793 it became a barracks, and a plan of 1862 shows hospital wards (the main house), 'cells' by the entrance, and other new buildings of military function. We have now reached phase IV, in the course of which it became a farm in the 1860s, and underwent further reconstructions (perhaps as a private house) in about 1906. Its final re-fortification was during the War, as a communications centre, with results that have reduced its archaeological potential considerably (phase V).

The materials are variously stone, brick, tile, and slate, with at least a dozen different mortar mixes recognisable.

Our principal concern is its alleged Roman origin. Roman bricks and possibly pottery are re-used in it, but neither this nor the oft-quoted herringbone masonry (in places) is a reliable indicator of date. One bastion is clearly hollow, another is solid—the latter being the fallen portion on the beach, where one must look to see the masonry in its earliest, unmodified, condition. Arguments from analogy with Roman forts and signal-stations are equally inconclusive (they are discussed on p. 50), and in the absence of a determined programme of excavation the matter must remain unresolved.

Numerous excavations have indeed taken place outside it, and earth-moving for the new sewage plant in 1979 was carefully observed. These have merely established that a ditch apparently does not exist, that the foundations are complex (with an offset), unmortared and about 1.3m. deep, and that there was a substantial settlement of Roman date nearby. The site of this last is unknown, though occupational material, several burials and masonry buildings with tiled roofs are recorded (p. 50).

The name 'The Nunnery' is supposed to be a soldier's jest, and the 'Hospital Wards' of 1862 may explain it. However, the 1735 document calls the fort 'Murs de Bas . . . formerly a convent'.

Publication: Kendrick's account (1921, 254–57) is full, but second-hand; for the fort and Longis Common generally *see* Johnston 1971 and 1977.

Burhou

> This offshore island is accessible only by boat. There is a single hut in which an overnight stay is possible with permission obtained in advance from the States of Alderney.

Two standing stones were supposed by F. C. Lukis (1847, 3) to be prehistoric, but they cannot now be found. Worked flints have been reported (Kendrick, 1928, 265–6) and an exceptionally fine blade of imported flint was found among the rocks in 1980 and presented to the museum.

OTHER ISLANDS

In addition to close offshore islands, such as Burhou (p. 135), Ile Agois (p. 83), Green Island (p. 74), and Lihou (p. 98), there are three reef-like groups that were accessible from the mainland and habitable in prehistoric times. Historically, they have been subject to territorial dispute between France and Great Britain. The French have retained the Chausey Isles as part of France, and La Grande Ile, with its 82 houses, two hotels, and a good harbour attracts some 100,000 visitors each year. The others, Les Ecrehous and the Minquiers, have remained British ('sans doute par negligence', as J. Doris tartly remarked (1929, 12n)), a claim settled by the Hague Tribunal in 1953. They are described by V. Coysh and M. Marshall in Coysh, 1977, 234–9. In practice they form part of the Bailiwick of Jersey. No archaeological material is known from Les Ecrehous.

Les Minquiers

Of about a dozen groups of outcrops exposed at high water, only one island, Maîtress Ile, has produced evidence of prehistoric occupation. (Godfray, 1929). The excavation identified two periods, separated by clean blown sand. The lower, of the Bronze Age, yielded pottery, flints and bones, mostly of grey seal, on what is thought to have been still a promontory of the mainland. By the Iron Age, Maîtress Ile may well have been an island, and renewed occupation was represented by three stone-built hearths, with pottery. One flagon-neck, probably Roman, and pottery of the 16th and 17th centuries have also been found. There is nothing to see today, and a recent inspection by the Société Jersiaise concluded that erosion has now removed most of the archaeological levels.

Les Iles Chausey

No archaeological investigation has been carried out on La Grande Ile. The first documentary reference is of A.D. 1022, recording the award of the isles to the abbey of Mont Saint Michel, followed by a sequence of monastic settlements with a church, and a priory from 1343. Several prehistoric monuments are recorded by Barhélemy (1973), including a 'sacrificial stone . . . with mysterious designs' near the chapel, a tumulus with a peristalith at La Pointe de l'Epée, other megalithic chambers at Grosmont, and a broken menhir with three or four chambers on La Gênetaie. Polished axes were found early in the 19th century by quarrymen in one of the chambers and are now untraceable (*see also* Marshall, 1965).

SELECT BIBLIOGRAPHY

Ahier, J. P., 1852. *Tableaux Historiques.*

Allen, D. F., 1971. 'The Sark Hoard', *Archaeologia* 103, 1971, 1–31.

Angel, J. L., and Coon, C. S., 1955. 'La Cotte de St. Brelade II: present status', *Annu. Bull. Soc. Jersiaise* 16, 1955, 301–6.

Baal, H. J., 1930. 'Report on the excavation of the Dolmen des Geonnais at Vinchelez de Bas', *Annu. Bull. Soc. Jersiaise* 11, 1931, 229–231.

Baal, H. J., and Sinel, J, 1915a. 'The exploration of a tumulus at Les Platons, Trinity', *Annu. Bull. Soc. Jersiaise* 8, 1915, 55–57.

Baal, H. J., and Sinel, J., 1915b. 'Exploration of "La Hougue Mauger"', *Annu. Bull. Soc. Jersiaise* 8, 1915, 58–61.

Baal, H. J., and Sinel, J., *et al.,* 1925. 'La Hougue Bie', *Annu. Bull. Soc. Jersiaise* 10, 1925, 178–236.

Barthélemy, G., 1973. *Les Iles Chausey* Publications du Pelican, Tartonne.

Bourde de la Rogerie, A, 1921. 'Un habitant de Sarnia, citoyen romain', *Rept. Trans. Soc. Guernesiaise* 9, 1921, 21–29.

Bruce-Mitford, R. L. S., 1956. 'A dark-age settlement at Mawgan Porth, Cornwall', in R. L. S. Bruce-Mitford, ed. *Recent Archaeological Excavations in Britain.* R.K.P., London.

Burdo, C., 1959. *La Cotte de St. Brelade, Jersey. Excavation of a Pre-Mousterian Horizon.* Société Jersiaise.

Burns, R. B., 1977. 'The late Iron Age site at the Tranquesous, St. Saviours, Guernsey', *Rept. Trans. Soc. Guernesiaise* 20, 1977, 188–218.

Cable, E. K., 1877. 'The excavation of the Beauport Cromlech, Jersey', *Annu. Bull. Soc. Jersiaise* 1, 1881, 324-326.

Cable, E. K., 1882. 'Memorandum of the excavation of the "Hougue" at Noirmont Warren', *Annu. Bull. Soc. Jersiaise* 1, 1881.

Cachemaille, J. L. V., 1928. *The Island of Sark,* ed. L. E. Hale, Reynolds, London.

Carey Curtis, S., 1912. 'An account of the discovery and examination of a cist or dolmen novel to Guernsey in October and November 1912', *Rept. Trans. Guernsey Soc. Nat. Sciences* 6, 1912, 401–414.

Case, H., 1969. 'Neolithic explanations', *Antiquity* 43, 1969, 176–186.

Chadwick, N., 1969. *Early Brittany,* Thames and Hudson, London.

Chevallier, R, 1976. *Roman Roads,* Batsford, London, 1976.

Clark, J. D. G., 1958. 'Blade and trapeze industries of the European Stone Age', *Proc. Prehist.Soc.* 24, 1958, 24–42.

Clark, J. D. G., and Piggott, S, 1965. *Prehistoric Societies,* Hutchinson.

Cliff, W. H., 1960. *Jethou: History, Flora, Fauna and Guide,* Guernsey Press Co.

Collum, V. C. C., 1933. *The Re-excavation of the Déhus Chambered Mound, Paradis, Guernsey,* Soc. Guernesiaise.

Cotton, M. A., 1954. 'Early Iron Age earthworks in Jersey', *Annu. Bull. Soc. Jersiaise* 17, 1958, 171–186.

Cox, J. Stevens, 1976. *Prehistoric Monuments of Guernsey,* Toucan Press, Guernsey.

Coysh, V. (ed.), 1977. *The Channel Islands: a New Study,* David & Charles, Newton Abbot.

Cunliffe, B. W., 1971. *Excavations at Fishbourne,* Soc. of Antiqs. Res. Repts., Nos. 26 and 27, London.

Cunliffe, B. W., 1978. *Hengistbury Head,* Paul Elek.

Darrell Hill, J., 1924. 'Report on the discovery of Neolithic ossuary at St. Brelade, Jersey', *Annu. Bull. Soc. Jersiaise,* 10, 1924, 79–89.

De Guérin, T. W. M., 1915. 'Examination of mound of dolmen of Le Creux des Fées', *Rept. Trans. Guernsey Soc. Nat. Sciences* 7, 1915, 192–193.

De Guérin, T. W. M., 1919. 'Notes on the recent discovery of a human figure sculptured on the capstone of the Dolmen of Déhus, Guernsey', *Rept. Trans. Guernsey Soc. Nat. Sciences* 8, 1919, 214–220.

De Guérin, T. W. M., 1921. 'List of dolmens, menhirs and sacred rocks', *Rept. Trans. Soc. Guernesiaise,* 1921, 30–64.

De Laet, S. J. (ed.), 1976. *Acculturation and Continuity in Atlantic Europe* (IV Atlantic Colloquium, Ghent, 1975) Dissertationes Archaeologicae Gandenses 16, Bruges.

Doris, J., 1929. *Les Iles Chausey,* Imprimerie Notre-Dame, Coutances.

Dunlop, A., 1896. 'On some Jersey peats', *Annu. Bull. Soc. Jersiaise* 3, 1896, 349.

Dunning, G. C., 1959. 'Anglo-Saxon pottery: a symposium', *Medieval Archaeol.* 3, 1959, 1–77.

Durtnell, C. S., 1930. 'Report on excavations in Alderney, May 1929–April 1930', *Rept. Trans. Soc. Guernesiaise* 11, 1930, 1–13.

Durtnell, C. S., 1966. 'The origin of the building known as The Nunnery', *Guernsey Evening Press,* 22 March 1966.

Ewen, A. H., and De Carteret, A. R., 1969. *The Fief of Sark,* Guernsey Press Co.

Finlaison, M. B., 1975. *A Preliminary Archaeological Survey for the Town of St. Helier,* Soc. Jersiaise.

Finlaison, M. B., 1976. 'A medieval house at 13 and 13a Old Street, St. Helier', *Annu. Bull. Soc. Jersiaise* 21, 1976, 477–493.

Finlaison, M. B., and Holdsworth, P., 1979. 'Excavations on the Ile Agois, Jersey', *Annu. Bull. Soc. Jersiaise* 22, 1979, 322–346.

Frend, W. H. C., 1956. 'Note on a Romano-British salt working at Chateau Rocquaine', *Rept. Trans. Soc. Guernesiaise* 16, 1956, 103–104.

Giot, P-R., 1960. *Brittany,* Thames and Hudson.

Giot, P-R. (ed.), 1979. *Préhistoire de la Bretagne,* Université Ouest-France, Rennes.

Godfray, A. D. B., 1929. 'Archaeological researches at the Minquiers, July 1928', *Annu. Bull. Soc. Jersiaise* 11, 1929, 193.

Godfray, A. D. B., and Burdo, C., 1945-50. 'Excavations at the Pinnacle, parish of St. Ouen, Jersey, 1930-36', *Annu. Bull. Soc. Jersiaise* 15, 1949, 21-100; 1950, 165-238.

Hawkes, J., 1939. *The Archaeology of the Channel Islands 2: the Bailiwick of Jersey,* Soc. Jersiaise.

Johnson, S., 1976. *The Roman Forts of the Saxon Shore,* Paul Elek.

Johnston, D. E., 1971. 'Archaeology study of the Nunnery', *Bull. Alderney Soc.,* Dec. 1971, 15–16.

Johnston, D. E., 1972. 'The re-excavation of the Beauport Dolmen', *Annu. Bull. Soc. Jersiaise* 20, 1972, 405–417.

Johnston, D. E., 1973. 'The Dolmen of Les Pourciaux South, Alderney', *Rept. Trans. Soc. Guernesiaise*, 1973, 301–306.

Johnston, D. E., 1974. 'The excavation of the Tourgis Dolmen, Alderney', *Rept. Trans. Soc. Guernesiaise*, 1974, 462–468.

Johnston, D. E., 1977a (ed.). *The Saxon Shore*, C.B.A. Res. Rept. 18, London.

Johnston, D. E., 1977b. 'Prehistory and archaeology' in Coysh, V. (ed.), 1977.

Johnston, D. E. (forthcoming). 'Megalithic communities of the Channel Islands', *Proc. Prehist. Soc.* (forthcoming).

Keen, D. H., 1975. 'Two aspects of the last interglacial in Jersey', *Annu. Bull. Soc. Jersiaise* 21, 1975, 392–396.

Keen, D. H., 1978. *Annu. Bull. Soc. Jersiaise* 22, 1978, 207.

Keith, A., 1912. 'A description of teeth of Palaeolithic Man, from Jersey'. *Ann. Bull. Soc. Jersiaise* 37, 1912, 225–40.

Kendrick, T. D., 1928. *The Archaeology of the Channel Islands 1: the Bailiwick of Guernsey*, Methuen.

Langouet, L., 1977. 'The 4th-century Gallo-Roman site at Alet (Saint-Malo)' in Johnston, D.E. (ed.) (1977a), 38–45.

Latrobe, G. and L., 1914. *Guide to the Coast, Caves and Bays of Sark*, Guernsey Press Co., 1914.

Lemprière, R., 1980. *Buildings and Memorials of the Channel Islands*, Robert Hale.

L'Helgouach, J., 1979. 'Les groupes humaines du Ve au IIIe millénaire' in Giot, 1979, 155–320

Lihou, J. L., 1976. 'Gallo-Roman salt-workings in Guernsey', *Rept. Trans. Soc. Guernesiaise* 20, 1976, 22–25.

Lukis, E. F., 1974. 'The Lukis family of Guernsey', *Guernsey Soc. Review* 30, No. 3, 1974, 79–82.

Lukis, F. C., 1847. 'On the antiquities of Alderney', *J. Brit. Archaeol. Ass.* 3, 1847, 1–15.

Marrett, R. R., 1912. 'Further observations on prehistoric man in Jersey', *Archaeologia* 63, 1912, 203–230.

Marrett, R. R., 1913. *Man* 14, 4–32.

Marrett, R. R., 1916. 'The site, fauna and industry of La Cotte de St. Brelade, Jersey', *Archaeologia* 67, 1916, 75–118.

Marshall, M., 1965. 'The Chausey Islands', Rept. Trans. Soc. Guern. 17, 1965, 747-50.

McBurney, C. B. M., 1967. 'Preliminary report of the current programme of excavations at La Cotte de St. Brelade', *Annu. Bull. Soc. Jersiaise* 19, 1967, 222–224.

McBurney, C. B. M., and Callow, P., 1971. 'The Cambridge excavations at La Cotte de St. Brelade, Jersey—a preliminary report', *Proc. Prehist. Soc.* 37, 1971, 167-207.

McCormack, J., 1977. 'Note on the discovery of a celtic cross in St. Peter's', *Rept. Trans. Soc. Guernesiaise* 29, 1977, 167.

Monnier, J-L., 1979. 'Les premiers groupes humains en Armorique des origines au cinquième millenaire' in Giot (1979), 35–153.

Meiron-Jones, G. I., 1973a. 'The long-house in Brittany: a provisional assessment', *Post-Medieval Archaeol.* 7, 1973, 1–19.

Meirion-Jones, G. I., 1973b. 'Settlement and vernacular architecture in Brittany', *Vernacular Architecture* 4, 1973, 3–6.

Meirion-Jones, G. I., 1980. 'La maison longue en Bretagne', Part I, *Archéologie en Bretagne* 26, 1980, 41–57.

Mourant, A. E., 1931. *Earthquakes of the Channel Islands and Neighbouring Countries. A Seismological and Historical Account.* Soc. Jersiaise, 1931.

Mourant, A. E., 1933. 'Dolmen de la Hougue Bie. Nature and provenance of materials'. *Annu. Bull. Soc. Jersiaise* 12, 1933, 217-220.

Mourant, A. E., 1936. 'A catalogue of earthquakes felt in the Channel Islands. First supplement', *Rept. Trans. Soc. Guernesiaise* 12, 1936, 523-540.

Mourant, A. E., 1963. 'Stones of the Mont de la Ville passage-grave, Jersey', *Annu. Bull. Soc. Jersiaise* 18, 1963, 317-328.

Mourant, A. E., 1966. *Jersey Archaeological Sites,* Jersey Society in London Occ. Publications, No. 12.

Mourant, A. E., 1974. 'Reminiscences of the excavation of La Hougue Bie', *Annu. Bull. Soc. Jersiaise* 21, 1974, 246-253.

Mourant, A. E., 1977. 'The use of Fort Regent granite in megalithic monuments in Jersey', *Annu. Bull. Soc. Jersiaise* 22, 1977, 41-9.

Nicolle, E. T., 1924. 'Discovery of a beehive hut at La Sergenté, St. Brelade', *Annu. Bull. Soc. Jersiaise* 10, 1924, 67-71.

Nicolle, E. T., and Sinel, J., 1912-1914. 'Archaeological researches at La Motte', *Annu. Bull. Soc. Jersiaise* 7, 1912, 241-245; 1913, 289-305; 1914, 450-451.

Oliver, S. P., 1870. 'Report on the present state and condition of prehistoric remains in the Channel Islands', *Journ. Ethnological Soc.* N.S. 2, 1870, 45 sq.

Ranwell, D. S., 1975. 'The dunes of St. Ouen's Bay in Jersey: an ecological survey', *Annu. Bull. Soc. Jersiaise* 21, 1975, 381-391.

Renfrew, A. C., 1973. *Before Civilisation,* Jonathan Cape.

Renfrew, A. C., 1976, 'Megaliths, territories and populations' in De Laet (1976), 198-219.

Renouf, J. T., and Urry, J., 1976. *The First Farmers in the Channel Islands,* Jersey.

R.I.B. Collingwood, R. G., and Wright, R.P., *Roman Inscriptions in Britain I: Inscriptions on Stone,* Oxford, 1965.

Rybot, N. L. V., 1924. 'Grosnez Hougue', *Annu. Bull. Soc. Jersiaise* 10, 1924, 72-74.

Rybot, N. L. V., 1932. 'The Dolmen de Faldouet', *Annu. Bull. Soc. Jersiaise* 12, 1932, 73-85.

Rybot, N. L. V., 1934. 'The surviving menhirs of Jersey', *Annu. Bull. Soc. Jersiaise* 12, 1934, 336-346.

Rybot, N. L. V., 1952. *Armorican Art,* Soc. Jersiaise.

Sanquer, R., 1977. 'The castellum at Brest (Finistère)' in Johnston (1977), 45-50.

Sanquer, R., and Galliou, P., 1972. 'Garum, sel et salaisons en Armorique Gallo-romaine', *Gallia* 30. 1972, 199-223.

Sinel, J., 1909. 'Submerged peat forest beds of the Channel Islands', *Rept. Trans. Guernsey Soc. Nat. Sciences* 6, 1909, 23-33.

Sinel, J., and Nicolle, E. T., 1912. 'The prehistoric cave-dwelling "Cotte à la Chèvre"', *Annu. Bull. Soc. Jersiaise* 7, 1912, 209-212.

Stevens, C. G., 1975. 'The Roman pillar in St. Lawrence's Church, Jersey', *Annu. Bull. Soc. Jersiaise* 21, 1975, 343-347.

Twohig, E., 1977. 'Megalithic Art in the Morbihan' in *L'Architecture Megalithique* Château Gaillard, Vannes, 173-186.

Wedgwood, W., and Mourant, A. E., 1954. 'The megalithic structures at the Jersey Gasworks', *Annu. Bull. Soc. Jersiaise* 16, 1954, 148-160.

Willy, F. J., 1964. 'Excavations at Frémont', *Annu. Bull. Soc. Jersiaise* 18, 1964, 367-370.

Zeuner, F. E., 1940. 'A new subspecies of red deer from the Upper Pleistocene of Jersey, C.I.', *Annu. Bull. Soc. Jersiaise* 14, 1940, 27-30.

Zeuner, F. E., 1946. 'Cervus elaphus jerseyensis, and other fauna in the 26-ft. beach of Belle Hougue cave, Jersey C.I.', *Annu. Bull. Soc. Jersiaise* 14, 1946, 238-254.

INDEX

141